When Love Wasn't Enough:

Because I Loved Him

Debbie Terry

Carpenter's Son Publishing

Published by Carpenter's Son Publishing, Franklin, Tennessee

Published in association with Larry Carpenter
of Christian Book Services, LLC
www.christianbookservices.com

Scripture is used from the New King James Version, © 1982 by Thomas Nelson, Inc. All rights reserved. Used by permission.

Scriptures marked KJV are taken from the KING JAMES VERSION (KJV): public domain.

Scripture quotations marked (AMP) are taken from The Amplified Bible, Old Testament. Copyright © 1965, 1987, by the Zondervan Corporation. Used by permission. All rights reserved.

Edited by Ann Tatlock

Cover design by Mary Balas

Author photo by Laura Payne

Interior design by Suzanne Lawing

Printed in the United States of America

978-1-952025-8-53

CONTENTS

Prologue 5

Chapter 1: Dream Guy 9

Chapter 2: Who Did I Marry? 43

Chapter 3: The Web Others Weave 59

Chapter 4: Our First Blessing 83

Chapter 5: Leaving Isn't Always Easy 89

Chapter 6: Our Second Blessing 99

Chapter 7: New Hope Dawns 111

Chapter 8: The Big "C" 127

Chapter 9: A New Life Without You in It 147

Chapter 10: Fighting for the Truth During
Alienation 161

Chapter 11: Something from Nothing 179

Chapter 12: Happiness and Abundance 197

Chapter 13: Getting Rid of the Demons 209

Chapter 14: Reflections 219

Chapter 15: Forgiveness 223

Chapter 16: Peaceful Blessings (Healing Heart and
God's Blessings) 231

Note From Author:

While dealing with this trauma I built walls of protection. My stance was made, then God began to tear down my walls and remove fear and anger. As God began to walk me through memories of it all again, I told him that I could not live through it another time. Then the love of God filled my heart with a new love and new peace and new faith to restore my soul, mind, and hope. Glory to God who gave me grace to settle the past and live in freedom that only comes from Him! I now live a peaceful, happy, and joyous life regardless of present or future trials. (May you find the same freedom.)

Prologue

I was at the lowest point I'd ever been in my life, and I didn't think things could get any worse. Twenty years earlier I had married the man of my dreams and had been more than ready to step into my new, fairy-tale life. Now I was beginning to realize that not only was the fairy tale ending, it had never even really begun.

Richard and I were in the midst of a divorce. It was a long, drawn-out, fiery divorce, fueled by his alcoholism and his lies. In our years together we had had two beautiful daughters, the joy of my life, but Richard, through his lies, was managing to turn them against me. He had almost succeeded in alienating them from me altogether. In fact, he had custody of our now teenaged daughters, and I was having to pay him child support. That was a struggle. Living alone and working as a Realtor in the middle of a recession, I was financially unstable and had so far been unable to find a second job to help pay the bills.

I was trying hard to hold on to God and my faith in Him. I read the Bible and prayed daily and trusted that He was walking with me through all this. One way He ministered to me was through my friends. Many of them were praying faithfully for me. Many invited me to get away for a while and spend time with them. I was overwhelmed by people's goodness to me and was constantly encouraged by the people God had put into my life.

But then came the day when things turned even worse.

On this particular day, I was visiting my friend Wendy in Atlanta, Georgia. She had invited me to fly down from my home in Nashville to spend a week with her, and I had eagerly accepted. Only recently, I had been so emotionally overwhelmed I had completely broken down physically and ended up in the ICU for three days. I needed to get away from the stress of my life and spend time recuperating. Being with Wendy afforded me the opportunity to rest, watch TV, and shop with a friend.

We were just about to leave to go shopping on that morning when my phone rang. I was headed down the stairs in Wendy's home when I paused to look at my cell phone. The call was from my home area code, but I didn't recognize the number. When I answered, I was greeted by a somewhat familiar male voice, but I couldn't really place him. It was disconcerting to think that I didn't know who this caller was, but worse than that, what he told me made me drop to the stairs in shock. I couldn't believe what I was hearing. My husband had been living a double life, and it was worse than I could ever have imagined …

Chapter 1:

DREAM GUY

My story begins after high school when I moved to Nashville, Tennessee, in 1989 to start my life. To pay for my gas, car payment, and rent, I worked as an administrative assistant doing clerical duties from 8:00 a.m. to 4:30 p.m. daily with a second job at the local grocery store various evenings during the week. I also had a third job at a jewelry store on Saturdays. Stacie, a friend attending college nearby, stayed with me from time to time. This story begins on an evening like any other as I came home from work to start supper. I walked up to the apartment mailboxes and met a young man, Ben, living upstairs from me. Little did I know that, later that evening, I would call on my new neighbor for help.

This particular night, as I sat down on the edge of my waterbed, the frame suddenly broke apart, allowing the vinyl mattress to spill out over the side. I jumped up and tried to grab it, but the mattress, filled with water and weighing hundreds of pounds, only molded itself around my hands. Other than that, I couldn't budge it. A leak in the mattress could become a nightmare, so I needed help. It was at that moment that I remembered the guy from the mailbox meeting. I asked Stacie to run up to Ben's apartment to get some help. Hearing their laughter from the doorway a few minutes later, I looked down and realized that the mattress wasn't the only thing falling out; I quickly adjusted my tank top.

Mystery man Ben fixed my bed and went back to his apartment. As the days went by, Stacie and I began spending more time with him. Ben came to dinner often, and the three of us would go out together. Soon he was dating Stacie. I began to feel like a tagalong, so I eventually sent them out alone. Besides, I didn't have much time for a social life. In addition to my three jobs, I also drove an hour and a half to my hometown almost every weekend to visit family and friends.

Still, at 19, I really wanted to laugh and share my life with someone special. Before moving to the city, I had had a first love. The young man and I were in a long-term relationship and planned to marry. Instead, we broke up and my dream was destroyed. Since then, I'd kept myself guarded and untrusting, not wanting to be hurt again.

My one dating experience after that was with a coworker who ended up moving way too fast. After only two dates, he decided he wanted to marry me. I told him that I didn't feel the same way and suggested we just be friends, but he had decided that I was "The One." The next weekend after my visit home, I met Ben at the apartment steps and he told me about a guy in a car that had been hanging around. The thought filled me with fear. I told him the story about my coworker, and Ben dealt with the situation for me. He became a good friend and I felt protected knowing that he lived nearby and was watching out for me.

My inspiration for a perfect relationship was my grandparents. My grandma, unlike me, always said that she "never went without a boyfriend and never had trouble finding one." She ended up with a jewel in my grandpa. I hoped to do the same. I started going to a nearby church hoping to meet a nice guy but still without success.

Ben and I talked about how I felt I didn't have the best judgment in the area of dating. Ben declared he would find me a "dude" and knocked on my door one September evening with a blind date proposition. I was to meet the "dude" at a party in Ben's apartment over the weekend. Ben worked his delivery routes with Richard. He assured me that Richard was good-looking, but I wouldn't know much more about him before the party. This made me curious and excited. I trusted Ben's judgment, but I also knew that I could escape downstairs to my own apartment if things didn't work out.

When Saturday night arrived, I was so nervous that I changed my hair, makeup, and outfit several times before Stacie came down for me. I found out the party was mainly made up of Ben's brothers and their families. As the clock ticked away, I passed the time playing and laughing with all the children. I didn't drink because drinking made me feel out of control, and I got tipsy after one glass. I had picked up a different bad habit of smoking, though. It was more to calm my nerves than out of pleasure. I had quit a few times since starting at age 15 but was currently back on board.

There were four kids in my lap when the awaited knock came at the door. In walked a tall, dark-haired, good-looking "dude." I immediately had thoughts that I could marry him. I was shocked as I had never felt that way before. I tried to compose myself and smiled as Ben introduced us. We had only talked for a few minutes when Stacie came to get me to ride with her to pick up the food. When we returned thirty minutes later, I found out that he was gone. Ben told me that Richard had previous plans and couldn't stay. I was disappointed and assumed he was really not interested in me. I went back to my apartment to be alone. I was still feeling strange about the immediate feeling that I could marry a perfect stranger. Was that what they called "love at first sight"? That was very unusual for me.

Over the next few days, Ben and Stacie both assured me that Richard seemed interested, so I sent him my phone number via Ben. Ben and Stacie spent time with me as I tried to carry on without expectations of him calling. It was more than a week later that Ben came to my door with Richard's number. He explained that Richard was very busy, but he was interested in meeting again. I was nervous about calling him as I had never been the first one to call in a relationship. After three rings, a young girl answered and told me he wasn't available. I left a message and hung up. Several days later, Ben came to me again asking me to call Richard. Richard still wanted to talk and would be home that evening. I decided that if he was my "dream guy" I had to give it one more try. This time, his mother answered and told me that he had already gone to bed because he had to work so early the next morning. What a strange schedule! Maybe this was why he hadn't been able to get back with me.

That weekend, I came down with walking pneumonia and ended up in bed for the next six days. I had to miss work at all three jobs and slept most of the time as my cough syrup knocked me out. A few days into the sickness, on a Tuesday night, Richard finally called back. I had a gruff, squeaky voice but tried my best not to cough. I smiled in amusement when I found myself primping as if he could see me. Richard apologized for his crazy work schedule. He went to bed early each night as he started his delivery shift at 2:00 a.m. He explained that he was off on Wednesdays and asked if I would be available tomorrow for lunch. I told him that I was normally at work but was off this week due to sickness. We talked a while longer and arranged for him to pick me up and go to a nearby restaurant.

After a restless night, I tried to cover my pale skin, red nose, and puffy eyes with powder. I had a frizzy, spiral perm that badly needed a trim; but physically, I felt much better. I quickly tried to tidy up the apartment as the doorbell rang. I opened the door to see Richard dressed neat and casual with a big smile. I gave him the tour of the apartment, and we left in his car. We listened to "Freedom" by George Michael on his cassette player on the way to the restaurant, and I was happy thinking we already had something in common.

When we sat down at the table, Richard asked if I liked wine. I explained that I didn't drink, but that it might help my throat a bit. I also hoped it might knock the edge off of my nervousness. As I sipped the wine with my salad, I began to chatter more than normal and I felt more comfortable and relaxed. We talked, laughed, and had a great time. After lunch, Richard suggested we go by the duck pond to watch the ducks and then to the pet shop to buy his niece a birthday gift. I was so at ease with him and everything just felt right. This was exactly what I was hoping for, and I couldn't stop smiling and thinking of our next date together. As afternoon approached, he took me back to my apartment so he could get to bed early for work. He hugged me and asked if we could go out again on Saturday evening. He drove off with George Michael blasting from the speakers. I went to sleep dreaming of our real first date.

That Saturday, we went on a double date with Ben and Stacie to a nearby tourist town. I wore my one-piece MC Hammer jumpsuit with black flats, and Richard sported his acid-washed jeans with a dress shirt and white sneakers. We took a picture on the apartment steps. On the drive to town, I rode in the front with Richard, while Ben and Stacie sat in back. Once there, we spent the evening visiting the street shops and eating together. Stacie suggested we get our picture made at Old Time Photo Shop. For the black-and-white photo, Stacie and I dressed up as saloon girls with guns in our garters while the guys dressed as cowboys with rifles. The photographer told us not to smile, which was hard for me. What memories! I learned so much about Richard that evening, and we laughed and enjoyed being together. Our first real date was a success.

The next few weeks, we spent Tuesday nights together, mostly watching TV with Ben and Stacie at Ben's apartment. This was the only night Richard could stay up later. Richard had previously made plans for the next several weekends with a high school friend named Jezebel. They were going to clubs where you had to be 21 to get in, and I was only 19. It seemed to me that Jezebel planned to exclude me by always picking places that I couldn't go. One day Richard asked if I wanted to meet her. On the way there he warned me not to take her the wrong way. She and her daughter were out on the porch when we arrived. When Richard went inside with her to talk for a minute, another high school friend, Teddy, arrived. I could tell by his actions and demeanor that he was gay. I wasn't bothered by this as I had two gay friends from my hometown. Teddy and Richard went off to talk as I sat on the porch with Jezebel. I tried not to judge Jezebel based on my first impression, but this was not easy. She seemed to be protective of Richard, but also a little threatening and jealous. It was like she was playing a game with me. On our way home, I wasn't very honest with Richard about my conversation with Jezebel. I tried to give her the benefit of the doubt. I also decided not to be suspicious of her, figuring that if Richard wanted to date her, he wouldn't be out with me. Later that evening, Ben and Stacie came to see how the day went, and I did open up to them about Jezebel. They both thought she didn't want to share her friend.

The following weekend, Richard planned to take me to a dance hall bar called Cadillac. He was going to a wedding earlier in the day with Jezebel, so we wouldn't leave until 6:30 p.m. Ben had been teasing me about "getting laid." I assured him that we had not been dating very long, and that my grandma always said, "If you give away the milk, he will never buy the cow." Ben just liked to get me riled up. I watched TV as I waited for Richard. Seven o'clock and eight o'clock came and went. Ben and Stacie came back from their date at 9:30. I waited until 11:30 before going to bed as I had to work the next day. No word came from Richard.

I had a message from Richard on my answering machine when I got home from work the next day. He said he had had too much to drink at the wedding and couldn't drive home. He also had no way to call and let me know. I had seen Richard drink only a couple of beers, and he said he didn't drink much after he left the military. Stacie assured me that he didn't seem like a drinker and probably just got into the wedding festivities. I was sure she was right as I drank a mixed drink every now and then, and it only took one to make me tipsy.

On Monday, Richard called and then came by to see me at my apartment. He told me about the wedding, and how he had to ride on horseback to the ceremony. It had been a horrible ordeal because he'd been given the only horse that wasn't properly broken in. Plus, the wedding was out in the middle of nowhere and once he got there he was stuck for the whole evening. I assured Richard that I was okay and I understood that he couldn't get in touch and had to miss our date. We talked for a while before he had to leave to go to bed. He turned to lean down and kiss me. It was a sweet, gentle peck; but it surprised me, and I smiled. Our first kiss! I felt like I was floating as I walked around the apartment thinking of what just happened.

We scheduled a date at my apartment for the next Tuesday night. I decided to make him dinner to save us some money. My grandma had given me some homegrown canned green beans, corn, and potatoes. I also made a batch of cornbread. My efficiency apartment had a kitchenette with a small table and chairs at the end of the bed, a dressing room, a closet, and a bathroom. The layout was small but less to heat and cool. Richard lived at home with his parents who were thinking of building a new house.

As he left, he invited me to a get-together at Jezebel's with her family on Saturday. I was hesitant to accept, but I knew it would give us a chance to spend more time together. He kissed me again and hugged me. It was at that moment that I knew he was definitely the one for me. He seemed like such a kind, mature, responsible dream guy. I laid in bed thinking of what the future would bring for us.

The next week was a whirlwind. On Saturday I was to meet Richard at Jezebel's after work as he needed to help her prepare for the party. When I pulled up at Jezebel's, Richard met me at the car smelling of beer. I didn't drink and definitely didn't have a taste for beer. He told me he had a few beers while getting things set up and didn't seem to act drunk. I dismissed any concerns because of the festive occasion. Jezebel stared at us as we walked into the yard, but I was immediately sidetracked by meeting all of Richard's friends and his sister, Hilda. Richard was the center of attention, the life of the party. Everyone was so nice to me, except for Jezebel who was very drunk. In addition to dancing and acting foolishly, she also made inappropriate physical contact with Richard at times. He laughed and told her to "cut it out." When I shared my concerns with him, he privately told me that she was always trying to get attention and that behavior meant nothing to him. Teddy showed up, and we talked for a while. As the night went on everyone continued to drink including Richard. It amazed me that he still seemed to function so well even when he was drunk. I asked him if I could take him home, but he informed me that he would stay the night there, and Jezebel would take him home after they picked up her daughter in the morning. He was very affectionate and wrapped his arms around me and kissed me goodbye.

The following weekend we went out alone. Richard took me to a huge, old house where there was an open dance floor, bar, and sitting area. We danced for a while and he left to go to the restroom. It seemed a rather long time before he returned and was ready to leave. We returned to the apartments and met Ben and Stacie in the parking lot. The four of us ended up watching a movie together, after which Richard hugged me and left. I felt very confused and puzzled and didn't have any time to talk to him privately. I think he felt the same way as he showed up the next day unexpectedly as I came back from church. We ordered pizza and sat together and laughed, just the two of us, uninterrupted, and it was nice. I realized that my love for him was growing deeper. I didn't speak my feelings as I thought he could surely tell by my actions and expressions. I hoped he was feeling the same way.

Several months went by, and we began spending time together through the week and on the weekends. Richard was spending all his time with me and taking me to places other than bars. One night I asked him to stay over at my apartment rather than drive home as he'd had too much to drink. That was the first night we were romantic together. I was very nervous even though it wasn't my first time sleeping with a man, but then a glass of cold water fell off the shelf at the head of the bed and spilled all over us! Talk about a shock! This broke the tension and had us laughing. I had been in one other long-term relationship earlier in my life, but I seemed to feel something special this time that I hadn't felt before. We laid together and talked for a long time. I told him about my other relationship, and he shared about his life and experiences around the world. He shared that he felt sex was overrated and wasn't everything to him in a relationship. A relationship was more than that. He also told me that he had fallen in love with me and called me his Tennessee Angel. I wasn't sure that we made the right decision to sleep together that night, but I knew then that I would marry this man. I smiled and thanked the Lord for sending me someone who would truly love me.

The next morning, I traveled back home and began to tell my mother more about Richard. My family knew we had dated, but now I decided it was time to let them know how I felt about him. Strangely, after I returned to the city, I didn't hear from Richard for several days. When he called, he told me that he had plans with Jezebel for the weekend as she was graduating from college. They were going to "over 21" places again, so I couldn't be involved. I had already planned the weekend off to spend with him and was again confused that Jezebel could still be trying to divide us. We seemed distant talking that week with neither of us saying "I love you" at the end of the phone calls.

The following weekend, Richard and I went out with Ben and Stacie on Saturday and ended up at a bar where Richard knew the bartender and bouncer. That way they let us all in. I was the designated driver that night, so the others had several drinks. We had a great time dancing, then Richard excused himself. He didn't return after a while, so Ben and I went looking for him. Neither of us could find him. When he eventually came back to the table, he said he had been out talking to a guy and time slipped away from him. I was upset and ready to leave. I didn't talk on the way back. Richard passed out when we got back to the apartment, so I talked a bit about the evening with my friends. I then called my brother who assured me that

Richard couldn't have been cheating on me in that amount of time. I didn't tell him about the other time it had happened, as my brother was very protective, and I didn't want to turn him against Richard.

The next morning Richard got up and went home, giving me a hug and kiss as he left. Jezebel called looking for him shortly after, saying they'd had plans the night before and he hadn't shown up. He left messages on my machine for the next few days while I was working and just showed up Tuesday with a card and some roses. He had never brought me flowers before. He signed the card "Love, Richard." I asked if Jezebel had found him. He said that they went out to celebrate Sunday night with her new boyfriend, and that she had acted up and annoyed him. With tears in my eyes, I told him that I wanted to address some of the issues we had been having. I was growing very tired of Jezebel and her actions. I was also annoyed with all the drinking, and the fact that he had been leaving me for long stretches of time on our dates without any excuse of where he had been. Even though I had fallen in love with him, I couldn't go on this way.

Richard began to open up and share his feelings with me. He said that he loved me, but had many stressful situations in his life that were pushing him to drink more. He told me about a previous relationship with a girl he almost married. They did drugs and alcohol together, and she had mental health issues. After the breakup, he left for the military in California and never planned to return to the area. Then his sister had an accident, and he came back to help. After moving back home, he was constantly at odds with his dad who was verbally and sometimes physically abusive. He had no privacy at home with his parents and siblings there. His one hope lay in the fact that they were building a new house and were planning to sell his childhood home to him when they moved out. As for Jezebel, she knew how he felt about me and was trying to separate us lately out of jealousy. He denied ever being intimate with her and claimed they had only been friends. Because of their long-term friendship, he was planning a good time to talk to her about all of it, a time when she was more rational.

This talk satisfied many of my concerns. I now understood why he had not introduced me to his family as well. After several hours passed, he got up to leave, and we kissed more passionately than ever before. It seemed like he wanted to say more, but was holding something back. This seemed to be a pivotal moment for us. I knew I still loved him and wanted to move forward in the relationship, but I wasn't sure what he would decide after hearing my concerns and expectations. I would wait to see how things went after he thought it over.

The following Tuesday, he showed up smiling at my door and reached out to pull me into a passionate embrace right there in the hallway. I felt like nothing in the world mattered but this moment. We went inside and made love then ordered pizza to be delivered. That evening we talked and laughed together, and he decided to take the next step to meet my family. My mom had scheduled a family picture at 3 p.m. on Saturday, so he would spend the night with me and go to work, then we would travel together to my hometown.

He called several times that week and genuinely seemed happier and lighter than he had before our talk. Everything went as planned. Richard met my mom and dad. My brother Al gave him the firm handshake and look that said, "You better treat my sister right, or you will deal with me." The two of them got along great at a local party later that night. Richard became a hit when he brought in a 12-pack of Michelob beer. Standing in the kitchen that day with my mother, I remember her commenting on his good looks and that he seemed to be a nice guy. Then she said, "He seems to be too good to be true. He may be either a cheater or gay." This was an odd comment from my mom who was a Sunday school teacher for over 25 years. I took it jokingly, and we both laughed. Richard and I slept in separate rooms that night at my parents' house and headed back to the city in the morning.

The next Tuesday night I made Richard home-grown veggies again, only this time with pork chops. I had cut back to two jobs which gave me more time home in the evenings. Richard began spending the night more often. The next weekend we planned a trip to the lake, and I would be picking Richard up as his car was in the shop. One street away from his house, my car broke down. I had to ask a nearby resident to use the phone to call him. He and his dad came to get me in a truck to tow the car. His dad was rude and standoffish and seemed annoyed and stern with Richard. I had to sit between them on the short drive to the house.

I was chattering nervously when his dad interrupted and said, "You don't know my son, or you wouldn't be with him. He's been in trouble, and he's not who he says he is. He's been into drugs and all kinds of things."

I was shocked by this comment but immediately said, "Sir, no disrespect, but I love your son, and I'm with him because I love him. So, who he used to be doesn't matter."

He laughed and said, "Suit yourself. I tried to tell you."

I was so glad to get out of the truck knowing how embarrassing that must have been for Richard. We stopped at a small rancher house where Richard's two younger siblings ran out to meet us. They were several years younger than him. His mother seemed sweet though childishly shy and giggly. The car problem ended up being a loose battery cable, and we were back on the road in a flash. Richard apologized for his dad's behavior. I could hear bitterness in his tone. I took his hand and squeezed it, explaining that he was the one that I loved, and it didn't matter. We went on to the lake for a great day of scenery and storytelling. Richard told me of cars at the bottom of the lake and a tower that was now underwater.

Once we were back at my apartment for the night, he talked more about his family. He told of his mom's personality changing over the years from his dad's influence. He asked if I would go with him to see his older sister Hilda the following day before I took him home.

The next day when we visited Hilda, she made us lunch and we spent the afternoon with her. She wanted to introduce me to Tarot cards, but it made me feel unsettled. I dropped Richard off at home. He kissed me, and I headed back to my apartment feeling content and in love.

After work Monday, my friend Katie and I went to look at a two-bedroom apartment that we could share. It would give us more room and save us both money. It ended up being perfect except for the fact that we had to climb many stairs to get to it. Thankfully, we were young and strong. We could move in after Christmas.

Richard and I had been dating for eight months that December. I had a special ornament made for us and hung it on a small tree on my dresser. I bought him a gold rope chain with a gold pendant, and he gave me a diamond and sapphire ring.

Richard spent less and less time with Jezebel. Ben and Stacie invited us to a New Year's party which was a large event. My sister and brother were invited, so I spent some time talking to my sister about some of her concerns. Mostly she was worried about Jezebel and Richard's drinking problem. I explained to her that Jezebel was fading out of the picture and that Richard didn't have a drinking problem. He drank a twelve-pack over the weekends and one or two beers on Tuesday nights. This seemed sensible to me, so I thought that she was trying to cause trouble. Richard also assured me that he did not have a problem.

Katie and I moved into the new apartment in January. I also took in a rescue dog about that time, a cocker spaniel named Blondie, whom we kept inside. I had an apartment key made for Richard who began to stay over most nights, as did my brother Al. Richard and Al had become friends and in fact had formed a tight bond, almost like brothers. Katie also liked Al.

My mom and sister came by to visit one weekend when Jezebel made an unexpected visit. Later, my mom called with great concerns about Jezebel. Mom didn't interfere much and usually had a lighthearted tone when talking with me about Richard. Now she seemed very sincere about not trusting Jezebel and her intentions. I told Mom not to worry because I didn't see Jezebel as a threat. I felt that if Richard wanted to be with her, he'd had years of opportunity for that. Richard had assured me that he would never consider dating her and that they would always only be friends. I can look back and see my simple "love is blind" attitude.

The next weekend, we all decided to throw Richard a surprise birthday party with the help of Hilda. Al and his girlfriend picked up Richard and me for a double date. It was a big surprise for Richard when we stopped by Hilda's apartment and everyone was there.

I expected social drinking at the party, but Richard and Jezebel became extremely drunk and started dancing on the coffee table inappropriately. I tried to pull Richard down as he tried to pull me up on the table. Jezebel made a scene about me not understanding their friendship; she claimed she was the one who knew what he needed. At this point I almost lost my cool and wanted to put my fist through her face. Richard pulled me to the side to apologize and help me calm down rather than ruin the party. We all ended up staying the night there. Jezebel brought her boyfriend into our room and made a scene on the floor next to our bed. By then I'd had enough. I left Richard passed out on the bed and slept in the living room chair.

The next morning, I told Richard that I wasn't willing to put up with that behavior from Jezebel any longer, and that he must make a decision. Hilda agreed with me. Before we left, she brought out her tarot cards again. I really didn't understand any of it, but I allowed her to read my cards. She flipped over many cards including "death," which scared me a little. Then she flipped a card and showed Richard privately. She stopped and said, "That's all for now." I was curious, but she wouldn't show me the card. She asked if I could be pregnant, and I told her I had been on birth control for years. I had also had female issues since the age of 14 and had been told I might not be able to have children. I was exhausted and ready to head home.

One weekend, we double dated with an old girl-friend of Richard's and her fiancé. She and I spent much time out on the porch talking about Richard. Strangely, I felt very comfortable around her, almost like an instant friendship. She and Richard had never been intimate, and she could only see him as a friend now. They met when he returned from the military, but the spark was no longer there. She was actually much in love with her fiancé and ready to be married. She knew Jezebel from the past and confirmed the things that Richard had talked about. She knew that he did not want a relationship with Jezebel, but that she had pursued one with him and wasn't to be trusted. She considered Jezebel jealous and needy. I really felt the evening was informative.

Richard began drinking more than usual, through the week and on the weekends. He and my brother would go out clubbing and out on the town. He continued to compare himself to other heavier drinkers as though to prove he didn't have a problem, but at the same time his drinking didn't slow down.

On the Saturday before July 4th, we awoke to sirens and found that our cars had been robbed and vandalized. The thieves had taken radar detectors, tapes, and change, as well as the mirrors off the sides of my sportscar. Richard's car was the only one that had been spared as it was an older model car. It was a long weekend for all of us, so we lounged around the pool to try to relax and recover from the theft. I wasn't feeling well with some menstrual cramping that I had from time to time. I'd had surgery in the past for a ruptured ovarian cyst and endometriosis. My periods could be painful, so I went in to lie down while the others stayed at the pool. After a while, the pain increased, Al ran to the store to get some Midol.

Richard came in to sit with me while Al was gone. I didn't tell them how bad I felt as I had been through severe pain before. Even with the Midol, I was getting worse. I was curled up in a fetal position with stabbing pain in my stomach. I staggered to the bathroom with uncontrollable cramping. In a few moments the toilet was filled with blood. I was about to black out when Katie came in the room. She went to get the guys. I convinced them that I could not afford an ER bill so they helped me back to the bed. I slept off and on but I had to get up to go back to the restroom again and again. There were huge blood clots and finally pieces of tissue mixed with the blood.

In the morning, I made an appointment with my OB/GYN, Dr. Howdy, and called my mom to come and take me. Dr. Howdy told me that I had a miscarriage, and that he needed to do a D&C procedure to keep infection from setting in. My mom was sitting in the lobby and had no idea what was going on. I was so full of emotions hearing that I had been pregnant and didn't know it. Now, I had lost the baby. I felt so empty and sad. Someone told my mom we were waiting on lab tests. After the procedure, she drove me back home. She stayed with me until Richard got off work. I was so broken and emotional that I could not talk for a while after he came. I didn't know what to say or do, so I asked Richard to give me some time alone for a few days. He left to stay with family as I fought with all my emotions and wondered what was to happen between us. Katie came in, and we cried together and talked until I fell asleep.

When I went back to work, I found myself trying to smile but ending up in the bathroom crying and feeling the emptiness and sadness. Richard called but I wasn't ready to talk. It was a week later when I called and asked him to come over. I didn't know what to expect as I almost felt abandoned by him even though I had told him to stay away. We sat on the couch together and, from his introduction, I felt that he was preparing to break up with me. I stopped him because I didn't feel capable of bearing the second loss. He laughed, and told me just the opposite. He actually had decided that he wanted to marry me someday. Still emotional, I felt that he only wanted to marry me because of the hurt and loss of the baby. I told him that I only wanted to marry because of love. He told me that love was the reason he would marry me. He then revealed to me that he had already bought me a ring. It was in his car the night of the vandalism, and he was glad it wasn't stolen. My heart just melted, and I cried and told him that I looked forward to spending the rest of my life with him.

The next two weeks went by smoothly. I was recovering well, and Richard had not been drinking or partying. I hoped that he would decide to put that life away as we talked much about marriage and hopefully a family blessed by God. The doctor had warned me that it might not be possible for me to carry children, and advised me against it for my safety. Richard knew this, too, and still wanted to marry me. He stayed with me for the entire week and, although we weren't intimate, I felt so close to him.

On our ten-month anniversary, Richard planned a dinner date for us on a river boat. I thought it was a double date, but to my surprise it was just the two of us. After dinner, we stood by the riverboat railing watching the water and shoreline. As we passed between the county lines, he pulled out the ring and proposed to me. I was stunned because I hadn't expected it to happen so soon. With excitement and tears in my eyes, I grabbed him and hugged him, almost dropping the box and ring over the railing. He had to ask me to marry him a second time, as I forgot to say "Yes!" the first time. My heart was so full of joy, and we were both so happy. We were going to be husband and wife! Our rocky road beginning had led to a fairy-tale, dream-come-true ending. I couldn't have been happier!

It was almost 1 a.m. when we arrived at the apartment. My roommate was waiting to congratulate us, and I called Mom to give her and Dad the good news. Richard and I had decided on a year-long engagement, but I went to bed with wedding plans running through my mind … a small old-fashioned church wedding. As we woke up together the next morning, I began to tell Richard my plans. He mentioned that he wanted to elope, but then relented and said we could have a small wedding. He thought it best to keep the expenses under five hundred dollars because of our many monthly payments, including the recent purchase of his childhood home. He wanted just the two of us in the ceremony, and I agreed.

We talked about wedding plans every night which helped keep my mind off the loss of the baby. I had a recent job change, and the boss's daughter had got married the week Richard and I were engaged. She offered me the use of any items from her wedding, including her veil and shoes (which were just my size). I planned to ask my friend Tess if I could borrow her wedding dress. My mother offered to make the finger food and table decorations. My parents also offered me five hundred and fifty dollars toward the wedding or a washer and dryer. We decided on the washer and dryer. We had been saving for a vacation together and decided to use our vacation money for more wedding plans such as the cake, plates, utensils, napkins, invitations, guest registry, paying the pastor, tuxedo rental, etc. We hoped to save some money during the year for a honeymoon.

I could see a change in Richard during this time. He seemed as happy as I was. My mother and his sister were planning bridal showers for me. Richard talked about plans to paint the walls of the house as soon as his family moved out. He wanted to paint all the rooms the same color. Richard took me, his fiancée, to meet his grandparents and his aunt. He seemed to have a great relationship with them all, and they were all so nice to me. As we ate dinner later that afternoon, Richard told me that Jezebel wanted to come over and see my ring and congratulate us. Although it shocked me that they were talking again, I didn't let it ruin our dinner.

The next day as I was putting groceries away, Richard scooped me up and set me on the counter and said, "Let's get married now, let's not wait." This totally surprised me as it had not been even a month since the engagement. I was so thrilled by this even though I still had a lease on the apartment, and his family had not yet moved out of the house. He said we would work it all out. The date was set for July 23, which was forty-three days away. That night was the first night after all that had happened that we were able to be intimate together. Everything felt so right. I couldn't wait to be Mrs. Richard Adams!

I called my mom the next morning to tell her about the changes. She immediately asked if I was pregnant, but I told her that we just didn't want to wait. We immediately started planning for the summer wedding. Richard planned for our picture to be made for the newspaper announcement. We placed an order for a small wedding cake and some simple invitations. Hilda held a lingerie shower for me, and my mom gave me a bridal shower. We got so many nice gifts for our new start together. Richard's family gave us a set of stainless steel pots and pans, some sheets and towels, a framed artwork of a local historical home, colored glass mixing bowls, fifty dollars, and some money to buy paint for the house. My grandparents gave us one hundred dollars, and my parents gave us the money for the washer and dryer. Many other friends and family gave us gifts to get us started on our new journey together. We planned to save the cash for our honeymoon.

I had the borrowed wedding dress cleaned and pressed. The veil and shoes were also borrowed. I received some white wedding hose and a satin ribbon garter at the lingerie shower. I had new undergarments also. My mom gave me a small blue handkerchief that belonged to my grandmother to wrap around the bouquet stem. A friend who was a florist would make my bouquet. Stacie, who was a beautician, would style my hair, and my dad would run the video camera. Richard's friend, a photographer, would take pictures and was including a photo shoot to be done in our future home. This was a surprise and would be my wedding gift to Richard. All our family and friends were such a blessing!

After that whirlwind week, we went to Jezebel's that weekend. We talked wedding plans for a while, and then Richard and Jezebel went off together in the car to talk. I wasn't worried this time as I knew that I was now his fiancée and soon-to-be wife. After they returned with some snack food, I noticed Jezebel glaring at me and looking like she was up to something. As we drove home, Richard announced that he wanted to add two people to our ceremony even though we had previously decided that it would only be the two of us. He told me that long ago he and Jezebel made a pact that they would be the best man or woman at each other's weddings. He didn't know how he could go back on his word. Then he told me that she would be wearing a tux. I told him that idea was completely absurd, and he must be drunk and crazy to even talk about such a thing. We argued until I told him there was nothing to talk about. Neither of us spoke for the rest of the return ride. At the apartment, Richard passed out and I couldn't sleep, so when Katie and Al came home, we went outside to talk it through. I ranted and vented about the insanity of the idea until I calmed down.

Richard was up the next morning drinking coffee with quite a hangover. The wedding was only three weeks away, and I felt like I had to take a stand. I would not have anyone making a mockery of our wedding. I hoped Richard would feel differently this morning, but he still said he would not go back on his word and argued Jezebel's point. I told him that no one would make our wedding a joke. Things were tense between us all day. His family had moved out of the house, so he went to paint. That evening I went over in tears and, after more arguing, I blurted out, "If Jezebel is in the wedding, I will not be there!" I left him that night not knowing what decision he would make. Why would he let her sabotage our wedding day? How could he see nothing wrong with this? Richard called when I got home and asked if I would talk to Jezebel. I agreed to talk to her so I could tell her myself that she would not be in the wedding. She called shortly after and tried to convince me of her plans. I told her that it would only be Richard and I in the wedding. She tried to twist and manipulate things to make it seem that I was being irrational. I then brought the fact up that Richard was not in her first wedding. She was not going to make me feel guilty, and she would not be in the wedding. She threatened me with a "We'll see" before she hung up. Of course, I didn't sleep all night.

I had to wait through a day of work before I talked to Richard. I explained my feelings again and told him that no woman anywhere would be happy with the idea he had proposed. He finally relented and agreed that it would only be the two of us in the ceremony. He wanted us to tell Jezebel together the next weekend, and I agreed. Meanwhile we busied ourselves with work, house painting, and wedding preparations through the week.

That Saturday was my private surprise photo shoot in our new home. Afterward, Richard went to pick up some beer and finger foods for Jezebel and her boyfriend's visit that evening. They brought along Teddy, who suggested we rehearse for the wedding since it was one week away. Jezebel, who was already drunk, immediately grabbed Richard's arm, and Richard looked at me. Teddy grabbed me and walked me around the side of the house before I could say anything. I explained to Teddy that this would not be accurate as Jezebel would not be in the wedding. He told me not to worry about it, and that she would accept what Richard told her even if she didn't like it. He also recommended that I have a ring bearer and flower girl. I thought that was a great idea! I had a nephew and niece who would both be perfect.

Teddy and Jezebel left shortly after that, and I returned to my apartment feeling much better. We would spend the next week apart as Richard finished up the house and I tied up a few loose ends. I just knew he would put me first now over others. My wedding day would soon be here, and we could start our life together as husband and wife. I would soon be Mrs. Richard Adams!

Chapter 2:

WHO DID I MARRY?

The wedding day had arrived! My beautiful white satin dress with short sleeves was waiting for me at the house, and my veil was in the car beside me as I drove anxiously to meet with Stacie who would be styling my hair and makeup. Suddenly, I saw blue lights behind me, alerting me to the fact that I was speeding. I was no stranger to getting pulled over in my little red, two-door sports car. Sometimes I ended up with a nice warning, and sometimes I got a nice, pricey ticket.

Today the officer approached my window to ask why I was in such a hurry. "I'm getting married today in a couple hours," was my honest response.

He chuckled as he took my license and registration. He chose not to ticket me as he told me, "You're getting ready to do far worse to yourself, and I won't add to it." He told me to slow down and get there safely, and I assured him I only had a mile to go. Then I sped off again. This would be a memorable moment to mark the upcoming occasion.

My Mom had everything decorated for the ceremony when I arrived at our future home where we would be married and living together as husband and wife. Mom looked as beautiful as ever in a stylish pink dress. We talked as Stacie worked on my hair. I wore it up beneath the wispy puffs of the veil with a crown of pearls at my forehead. Mom informed me that she had talked with Richard and felt better about our marriage. I had been on my own for about three years, so it seemed surprising that she would still be worrying about me and my decisions, but I took it as a sweet gesture.

Stacie put the finishing touches on my hair and makeup, and everyone left me to go get seated. I looked at myself in the mirror and sniffed back tears. It was hard to believe that everything was fitting into place and, in just a few minutes, I would be Richard's wife. I was pushing back memories from last night's rehearsal, which was more like a bad dream. Jezebel, Teddy, and a few others came over to celebrate and soon everyone was drunk. As Richard and I rehearsed, Jezebel tried again to stand in as the best man, making a scene. I tried to ignore her, but soon she and Richard were arguing with me about my decision. Once Richard sobered up, he realized that the idea was absurd. It was still difficult to go through this battle again the night before the wedding.

My mom opened the door which ushered me back into reality. There I was again in the mirror looking like a fairy-tale princess. I knew that I had made the right decision, and I would shortly be marrying the man I loved. I left the bad dream behind as I walked out the door with my heart full of joy.

Richard was so handsome in his black tuxedo as we exchanged our vows before all our family and friends. Not long after saying "I do," I located Richard and Jezebel drinking in the garage. Out of respect, we had decided to wait to bring out the alcohol until our parents and grandparents left the wedding. I didn't make a scene as I didn't want to spoil the day. The reception lasted well into the night and ended with Richard crashing in the bedroom as the guests left us alone for our first night as husband and wife. I was disappointed as I had dreamed of a romantic wedding night as a couple, sharing our love together. I at least had the consolation that there would be many more nights to come.

The next morning was the beginning of our honeymoon as we had the whole week off. After finding Teddy passed out in our garage, we gave him some coffee, and we were on our way! I couldn't wait to spend an entire week together, just the two of us! We were going to spend our first three days in a hotel in the mountains to stay in a honeymoon suite with a hot tub. We stopped at the liquor store to get some bourbon and the grocery store to grab some snacks and breakfast.

Upon arriving, we discovered that the reservation had only been booked for one night instead of three. After a protest, the hotel management added the additional two nights. Once we reached our room, Richard turned on the TV as I went into the bathroom to put on the sexy nightie and robe I had reserved for our wedding night. I came out and asked Richard if he liked what he saw. He just laughed and said that those things were silly because they didn't stay on very long. After his TV show was over, we made love. I was rather disappointed as it felt so rushed and not as sensual as I had imagined. We got in the hot tub for a little while, and then he got back out to watch TV.

That was when Richard told me of his other plans for the week. My expectations of a week-long trip with just the two of us sightseeing, being romantic, and staying in together were in for a rude awakening.

Richard announced that he had called an old friend from the military, David, and wanted to spend some of his time off visiting him. David lived in a remote area in another state. Richard wanted to go ahead and cancel the other two nights at the hotel and use the money for gas. Dismayed, I agreed to his plans. At least we would be spending time together.

We drove back home to repack for the new adventure. I did most of the driving to David's house as Richard was drunk. As we got closer, I noticed fewer and fewer houses as we drove farther away from civilization. Where would we eat or get supplies? I questioned Richard about this, and he said that David had taken care of everything we would need. Not long after, we pulled up to a small house where David was standing on the porch at the grill. I was then informed that we would be staying here for a week.

Trying not to worry and to trust my new husband, I smiled as we removed our bags and went inside. About an hour later, Richard informed me that he and David were going to run some errands. They would be taking my car, but there was a home phone if I needed it. The TV didn't have cable, so I picked up my book to read for a while. Surprisingly, there was food in the refrigerator, so I made a sandwich and read until I fell asleep. I awoke at 4 a.m. with no sign of the men. I felt so isolated and helpless. All alone, I began to cry and pray that nothing had happened to them. The car pulled up a few hours later. I was so scared and mad and awaited an explanation. Richard was clearly intoxicated and agitated when he walked into the bedroom telling me some story about getting lost and navigating back roads all night. He also had something white on his nose which he said was nothing. He passed out before my eyes, so I went into the other room frustrated, hurt, and confused. I just began to cry again, wondering how this could be happening on my honeymoon. Mentally and emotionally exhausted, I fell back to sleep.

There was no sign of David when I awoke. I needed an explanation from Richard, but he woke up angry and defensive. He actually tried to put the blame on me. Newlyweds or not, I had decided to get my keys and leave. I changed clothes and packed my bag, but the keys were nowhere to be found. The car was locked, so I went back inside to search again when Richard jumped up and grabbed me by both arms. The look in his eyes was a mixture of anger and fear that I had not seen before. He told me that I had to calm down because we were both in danger. He couldn't talk to me about it now, but he would explain later when we were alone. His look sent a chill down my spine. I suddenly wondered, "Who is this man that I just married?" I demanded that we go home, but David had the keys.

Richard said everything would be okay in a few days. A few days?!? I felt like I couldn't breathe, thinking about staying here in danger from an invisible enemy. Thoughts of being murdered in some godforsaken place in the middle of nowhere filled my mind. Why did Richard put me, his new wife, in a situation like this? There was nothing left to do but cry again.

Richard calmed down and put his arms around me, and we both laid down on the bed. David called Richard and said it was time to go. I quickly sat up as Richard jumped into his clothes. I was too scared to ask any questions. Richard told me to have him some coffee ready, leaned over and kissed me, and said, "I'll be back when we're through." Through with what? He then said that we would go out to dinner that evening, and they left. All I could do was sit and wait. I was so confused, but too afraid to call anyone as this was my new husband who was acting so suspicious. Also, I couldn't ask anyone to come pick me up since I didn't even know where I was. I watched some local TV and read again until the men came back about 6 p.m. Richard seemed quite happy, smelling like alcohol but not really drunk. I followed him into the bathroom as he got in the shower. As he showered, he told me it had all been a joke and that we were going to David's parents' for dinner. I stood there in disbelief and with mixed emotions. Was it really a cruel joke or a cover-up? I felt I had no choice but to get ready and go.

Richard would not talk to me about the events of the last forty-eight hours and told me to forget about it and drop it. David's family was very pleasant. I put on a smile while we visited them, but urged Richard to get the keys so we could head back home after dinner. I tried to keep trusting him, hoping he was making bad decisions to impress his friend. I knew I would feel better when we were heading home. Richard told me we would visit with David for a while, and then he would tell him we were leaving early. Instead, David took Richard with him to make a quick run to the store to get some beer. My gut told me that I would be spending a long night alone again. I packed my bag and then did some more reading until I fell asleep in the chair.

They returned in the early morning hours. Richard was acting hyped up rather than drunk. He pulled me out of the chair into the bedroom and started undressing me. I began to protest while he shushed me and laid me down in the floor of all places to have sex. He said it would be quieter, and we would have more room than on the twin bed. He acted so sensual and sensitive toward me, which had never happened before. I was shocked but enjoyed it. He didn't rush, and I truly felt his love for me like never before.

Richard passed out, and we slept together until morning. I got up and went in the kitchen to get Richard's coffee when I met David. He smiled and said, "Good morning. Did you and Richard have a good time last night?" Embarrassed by the question, I laughed and gave an awkward, "Yes." David laughed as he went in the bedroom and said, "I told Richard it would make everything okay." This was all just so weird that I couldn't wait to get out of there, put all of this behind us, and move on.

I was ready to leave with or without Richard, but thankfully he said he was "done here" and ready to go home. I didn't take time to ask what that meant; I just packed the car and headed toward the interstate. Tears fell down my face as I thought about the past few days. I was afraid to tell anyone what happened, thus beginning my years of covering up my husband's secret life. I realized there were things I didn't know about Richard, but I didn't question him as I felt like it would bring up all the hurt again. Richard convinced me that I had overreacted to the situation, and I agreed that I would put it behind us. I determined to put a smile on my face and get back to being a happily married bride and giving my marriage 100 percent.

We settled into newlywed life over the next few weeks. I finished moving into the house, leaving my brother Al to finish up my lease on the apartment. I left most of my furniture for him to use as we would be buying new furniture as we could afford it. We began furniture hunting right away. Knowing that we would need to make payments, we decided to pay off each furniture set before we bought more. We started with a bedroom suite. I found out we had very different decorating styles and price range ideas. Rather than arguing, I decided it would be easier to let him make most of the decisions. I wanted so much to make our marriage last forever as I believed in the phrase "until death do us part." My parents and grandparents had made their marriages last by morals and values and working together. On the other hand, my sister and brother had both been divorced. In my eagerness to please, I found myself in a cycle of codependency early on.

I was determined to be the best wife I could be. That meant keeping the house clean and cooking as much as possible. Richard had already instructed me on the proper way to do his laundry, and I was doing my best to launder everything to his liking. I used many coupons and bought whole chicken at the meat market to save money. I made chicken almost every night. My brother often joked that we would soon start looking like chickens. I struggled with getting all parts of the meal ready to eat at once. By the time the cornbread and potatoes were done, the chicken was cold. It would become tough when reheated in the microwave. One night, Richard hurt my feelings about this, so I told him he could cook his own meals. That was one moment I stood up for myself.

One day while cleaning the closet, I found some books on witchcraft wrapped in a cloth in the back corner. I was very shocked as I thought we both knew God. I didn't know how to bring up the subject, so I just decided to leave them out on the bed. Richard didn't volunteer any information. After questioning him, I discovered they belonged to his sister. I demanded that he get rid of them and didn't speak of it again, but I was very disturbed.

Our new schedule allowed us little time together, and our sex life became inactive. Most nights Richard was in bed when I got home from work. I spent much of my evening time alone crafting gifts for the holidays. We spent time decorating and landscaping on the weekends. We visited friends and relatives on Tuesday and Saturday nights. People began to notice a distance between us and, consequently, Richard flirting with other females, especially Jezebel. If I tried to talk to him about it, he accused me of being sex crazy or picking an argument. He felt that he was more mature and liked to be alone. He actually preferred not having sex, but he tried to make love to me when we had the chance.

We spent most of our free time with others, and partying became an every-weekend event. Richard referred to himself as "the life of the party." I usually kept the parties running as smoothly as possible, and afterward I cleaned up after everyone. Jezebel became a chronic intruder. If she didn't get the attention she wanted, she would pitch a fit and make threats. Many times I would come home to full-blown parties with everyone drunk, and often neighbors had to call the police for embarrassing situations. Many times, Richard was passed out or irrationally drunk. If I tried to discuss it with him, he would tell me that I needed to "let my bun down and enjoy life." Many days I wondered what I had done by entering this marriage, but I did not want to consider divorce.

At one point, Richard and Jezebel had a huge argument, after which he vowed to be done with her friendship and selfish ways. I felt greatly relieved, as I was sick and tired of all the partying and Jezebel's influence. It was so hard to watch the one you love being controlled and destroyed by another and feeling that you could do nothing to stop it. Also, the neighbors had been calling the police quite often because of the loud music and noise. I also felt like there was no end in sight, and my faith in God seemed to be wavering. I didn't understand why He would allow this to happen when all I wanted was a normal marriage.

The next few months were calmer and more peaceful. Although Richard was still drinking, he didn't seem to be getting drunk. I hoped that God was at work in him as I prayed for that so much. We even started going to church together on the weekends. One weekend, I decided to visit my family, but Richard had to work and couldn't go with me. He had invited Al over and gave me his word that he would not have a party. When I returned everything looked normal. Richard told me he broke a few glasses, but everything was clean and tidy.

A few days later when I was talking with a neighbor, the story came out. As we sat together, she hesitantly told me about a wild party at my house over the weekend and a half-naked girl rubbing her topless body up and down my glass storm door for the entire neighborhood to see. She tried to console me as I burst into tears. She knew that I probably wasn't home at the time as she had not seen me. She, of course, didn't know about our secret life as I kept it hidden from everyone. She also told me that the police had been called, and there was a loud fight between Jezebel and her own brother.

Embarrassed and angry, I was ready to leave and go to my parents' house. My love had not changed, but I was tired of overlooking his misdeeds and covering up for Richard. I was sick of the lies and deception and the reverse blame game. I felt like such a failure and even wondered if God was punishing me. As I was writing a note to tell Richard where I was, the phone rang. It was Richard's mother. She had heard about the party and was calling to talk to Richard. I told her that I was leaving, and she asked me to come by and talk to her. Before I could get my things in the car, Richard came home from work. With swollen eyes and a searing headache from all the crying, I went out the back door to get Blondie. Richard called to me from the front porch as I loaded the dog into the car. "Angel, where are you going?" He walked over and began to question me about why I was crying. I handed him the note to explain and left him standing confused in the driveway.

Richard's mother and I sat on the porch as I poured my heart out to her. She couldn't understand how I had lasted this long since we had been married almost a year. She told me that alcoholism runs on both sides of the family. Most of them, like Richard, could function in their daily lives even while drinking. All their wives seemed to suffer in silence, emotionally and financially. I knew nothing about alcoholism as my family had not experienced this. The friends and people I knew were only social drinkers who could quit when they wanted. His mother advised me to leave before I brought children into this lifestyle.

Looking back, I could see some of the red flags that I had ignored.

Richard pulled into the driveway but, on seeing me there, turned around and squealed the tires as he raced off. Shortly afterward, the phone rang, and it was him asking to talk to me. He was angry that I had gone to his parents with this problem. Then he told me I was overreacting and blaming him for something out of his control. I should just come home, and we could work it out ourselves. I was too angry to speak so I hung up. How dare he blame me for all of this! So many thoughts and so much confusion were running around in my head. The mental torment was unbearable. I went back and forth, accusing him and then accusing myself. Had I not been a good wife? Did I not satisfy him? Would I leave for good, or would I stay and fight for our marriage?

I decided to drive back home. I told Richard that I could not talk just then as my head was throbbing and I needed to sleep. I put Blondie in the backyard and went to the spare bedroom and cried myself to sleep. The phone woke me in the morning. I ignored it as there was no one I wanted to talk to now. My body felt heavy and weighed down, and the headache was raging. "What do I do now, God?" I prayed as I cried. My heart was breaking as I remembered the vows we made to each other ... vows before God, family, and friends. I did not take this lightly. I had committed myself to Richard "until death do us part." I knew that God wouldn't let me down as He was always faithful.

As I walked through the house, I felt a tangible sadness in the air. It seemed so empty and cold. Could happiness be gone so soon? I had truly given my best to make Richard happy, often putting my feelings and desires aside for his. I looked at my swollen face in the mirror and knew that I would be miserable if I left him and miserable if I stayed in these circumstances. I took a hot shower and put on fresh clothes. The phone rang and it was Richard. "Angel, I'm glad you're there. Could you stay home for us to talk when I get off work at noon?" I whispered an "Okay," and decided to read my Bible and pray about what to say and do. Noon would come soon enough.

Chapter 3:

THE WEB OTHERS WEAVE

The Bible was laying on the couch beside me when Richard came in and sat down. I had hoped to hear a voice from God saying "leave" or "stay" so I would have clear direction in this situation. Instead, I felt like I received comfort and strength for whatever would happen. Richard broke the unsettling silence. He apologized and told me that he loved me. He also admitted to going overboard and getting drunk and that the party got out of hand. Then he began to make excuses explaining that "everything started off with just having a few people over" and "it was all out of my control" and "we are young and need to have fun." I went back and forth from angry to compassionate. I was just ready for him to take some responsibility for his actions. I also needed him to see his problem with alcohol. He believed he needed to drink to get along with others and that he could stop whenever he wanted. After talking with his mother, I knew that this was a generational problem. I asked him if he would be willing to take steps to sobriety and focus on our relationship. I wanted him to agree to attend church more with me and put our marriage first. He said, "I love you, Angel, and whatever it takes for you to stay, I will do." I began to cry tears of joy as we hugged and held each other. I felt that, in time, God would heal our hurts and wounds.

Instead, I continued to lead a life of secrets and covering up for him with family and friends. I longed for a different life, tried to be patient, and constantly prayed that God would change Richard's heart and lifestyle. His drinking slowed down without all the parties and friends around.

Then one day I passed out at work and had to take a few days off. I was called into the boss's office and told they were letting me go because of health reasons. I had dealt with these episodes surrounding my menstrual cycle since I was 11 years old but, at this point, we decided I should see another specialist. My mom found one out of state, and she volunteered to take me and pay the cost to go. Richard was thankful for my mom's role in this as he didn't work well with sickness. I was put on a waiting list and was wearing a heart monitor and taking medication which required me to have constant supervision as the blacking out episodes were becoming more frequent.

Three weeks later, I kissed Richard goodbye, and my mom and I were on a flight to see the new neurologist. I tried not to worry about the money and insurance and all the tests they were running as I was told it was all covered under one payment plan. The neurologist met with us first in the morning and again in the afternoon to go over the test results. He determined that I likely had a form of epilepsy with petite mal seizures which were linked to the migraines I had been having since I was young. He also told me the great news about a new drug being used to treat this problem. I was so relieved to be going home in just three days with good news and hope to live a normal life.

With the seizures under control, I went back to school to get a degree to become a surgical technician and started a part-time job working for Teddy's mom doing secretarial work in her real estate office. In two years, I planned to graduate and start a full-time job in the medical field with guaranteed full-time income. Soon after I started, though, Richard approached me with an idea to change my career path and go to a nearby real estate school. The program was three intense months, but I could begin to make money much sooner. He had considered this for himself but could never make the time to go. Richard also offered to allow me to go to school without working for those three months. I felt like this was the right choice for us, so I quit my job and college classes and jumped right into it, going to real estate school all day and studying all night.

During this time, we took in an old friend of Richard's who was going through an abusive relationship. It turned out that she was also an alcoholic, which had contributed to her problems. Suddenly Richard started drinking more and the party life returned. I began to wonder if I had made a mistake by quitting my job, college, and my degree. Finally, the day came for me to take the state boards, and I passed! I called home to tell Richard. Teddy answered the phone, and I could hear the party going on in the background. When I arrived home, everyone was out in the backyard drinking and partying in their bathing suits. Richard stood up and announced through slurred speech, "Here is the new agent!" The backyard and kitchen were a disaster, and I found two kids unattended watching TV in the living room. This was nothing new, so I offered them some PB and J sandwiches. The kids were always happy to see me as their own mothers did not take care of them. Seeing the neglected children of these alcoholics made me almost happy that I had not brought a child into the world with Richard. The celebration lasted way into the evening and many guests needed transportation home because they were too drunk to drive.

The next few weeks were a whirlwind as I awaited my license. Teddy's mom had asked me to work for her office since I had already fit in so well. I also already had a client waiting for me to get everything in order and start my business. The day I was set to meet with him, I had a seizure, the first one since starting the new medication. Even though I felt better by meeting time, Teddy's mom sent me home and said she would "cover it for me." I cried all the way home, feeling betrayed. Richard made a few phone calls while I slept and he decided that I would clean out my desk and quit. I didn't know Richard was going to make those calls. He explained that it was best for me and no one would treat me that way again. I felt he was protecting me by making these calls. When I went back to the office, Teddy's mom was very rude and told me that I would "never make it in this business." I left crying and hurt. This episode also ended our relationship with Teddy and Jezebel (although I knew she would eventually come back). I was shocked by the way Richard stood up for me and put me before his friends. I just knew that this time things would change for the better.

We were in our third year of marriage, and the drinking was under better control again. I was working full time as a Realtor now after making a new friend named Liz who was also a coworker at my office. I was trained by my broker, Mr. Rule, who had been in the business for thirty years. He helped break down my soft, sensitive core, allowing me to deal with people of all personalities without taking offense and being hurt. This would give me strength in the business world. Richard claimed he liked the "old Angel" better as I began to be more vocal and stand up for myself and my interests more than before. I still gave Richard respect and did not want to push him too far.

My first year as a Realtor was spent working hard and proving my worth to stay in the business. I began to make a name for myself as someone who was service-oriented, honest, and people-friendly. I treated my clients as extended family and grew my business through hard work, long hours, and referrals. I found that if I didn't make the sale, I didn't earn a paycheck though I still had to pay for my fees and advertising. I tried to cut costs by taking my lunch and not making any unnecessary purchases. Richard paid most of the bills at this time, and we had to finance a second car for me. He put a large, red bow on it and gave it to me as a Christmas gift. This landed us with two monthly payments.

By my second business year, I was hardly home with Richard, and we began seeing less and less of one another. I thought he might ask me to slow down; instead, he wanted me to make more money so we could get ahead. We began talking about starting a family as we had now been married for four years. I still had my concerns because of the drinking and my past health issues and the miscarriage. I also felt that our intimate relationship was still shallow and without affection. I felt that Richard was a good guy apart from the drinking that caused the aggression and verbal violence. It seemed that he would go for several days living a normal life and then plunge into drunkenness and shut down. I continued to pray that God would remove whatever hindrance was in his heart that would cause this heavy burden. I just knew that if he would align himself with God's plan, everything would change.

My career helped me keep my mind off the problems at home. Working in real estate seemed like my dream job as I was able to make a living helping others. I also tried to focus on being thankful for the blessings in our lives. The new medication was keeping the seizures and migraines under control, and Richard and I had been going to church more. Just when it felt like we were moving forward in our marriage, I came home from work one day and there was Jezebel sitting outside with Richard, laughing and chatting away. Richard called me over and said, "Look who came by to see us out of the blue." I later found out he had called her and invited her over to drink with him. I wasn't happy about it; however, Richard assured me after she left that she had calmed down and would be better this time to us both. I wanted to believe she could change and felt as though I had to give her another chance. Besides, Richard had been such an on-and off friend to her for so long.

Later that week I came down with a stomach bug. After four days of vomiting, I called Dr. Howdy, my long time gynecologist, for an appointment. I had multiple tests done and went home to await the results. Richard was distant as usual when I was sick. He always said it was better for only one of us to be sick, so I would sleep in another room, and we would stay apart. After my doctor's appointment I spent a quiet afternoon in my backyard with Blondie. Our backyard was like a wooded paradise where you could sit and breathe fresh air and enjoy God's creation. Watching the wildlife was refreshing and peaceful.

The next morning, I felt better and went back to work. I got a call from the doctor's office and told Dr. Howdy how much better I felt. He laughed and said, "Angel, you don't have a bug or virus ... you are PREGNANT!" Standing up, putting my cigarette in the ashtray, I froze. "Angel, are you there?" Dr. Howdy asked.

My head was spinning and I was in shock. Was this for real? I heard him tell me that I needed to come back to the office so they could closely watch this pregnancy due to my health concerns and my medication. I left the office crying in joy and fear. How would Richard respond to this? Although we had talked about having a family, he also voiced his love of freestyle living without kids. I had even heard him talk about abortion as an option for people who weren't ready for children. I knew I could never abort a child as they were precious gifts from God. I knew my baby was a precious gift for me after losing my first child in the miscarriage. I was determined to raise this baby alone if necessary. My mind was racing as I drove around, processing the news. What would happen to my job? I had only been there a year. Would my broker see me as valuable enough to work with me through this? I knew I had to keep working as Richard had made this clear in the beginning of our marriage. Oh, and what about all the medications I was taking … would they harm the baby? I thought about my smoking and determined to stop immediately. I didn't even know how long I'd been pregnant, as it seemed like a long time since Richard and I were intimate. I decided to stop driving around and finally hurried home to tell Richard the news.

Richard was on the phone in the bedroom when I walked in the house. He abruptly got off and asked why I was home so early. Without waiting for my answer, he told me that he was feeling bad now and thought he had caught my virus. Laughing, I said, "You couldn't possibly catch what I have!" He wanted to go to bed and talk in the morning, which made me start to cry. I blurted out, "I'm emotional because I'm pregnant!" He immediately sat up in the bed. He looked puzzled and surprised as I began to explain everything to him. Richard sat in silence until I said, "Say something." He said, "I need a cigarette." My heart felt pierced as he told me he didn't think I could have children. He didn't grab me and hold me in joy as I had hoped; he just went out to the backyard to smoke.

I followed Richard and sat beside him on the glider, putting my arms around him. He asked how far along I was, but I didn't know as I had been taking my daily birth control all along. I had very irregular periods even on the birth control and had a tilted cervix. Part of my cervix had also been removed because of precancerous cells. Richard seemed worried and finally voiced his concerns that he was very drunk the last time we were intimate. What if the alcohol had affected the baby through his sperm? I had not thought of this. I just began to cry. So many fears were surrounding this pregnancy at a time I should be able to celebrate in joy. I asked Richard if he was on board for this pregnancy. Still in shock, he said that he was on board but wanted to wait to share the news with others because of all the concerns and the previous miscarriage. Though disappointed, I agreed to his seeming wisdom in this unsettling moment. I felt better knowing he would be by my side to raise our baby and decided to be excited about this blessing from God.

At my first high-risk appointment, we discussed my medications and a pregnancy plan. My OB/GYN Dr. Howdy and Dr. Rye, my neurologist, were prepared to work closely together for my management. They determined it would be better for me to stay on the epilepsy medication than take a chance of having a seizure while pregnant. Richard and I discussed it all over dinner that night, and we decided to tell the family on the weekend. My parents and grandparents were overjoyed! My mom immediately began talking to me about shopping for baby items. Richard's parents didn't react quite the same way. Although his mother congratulated us, she pulled me aside to ask, "Are you sure about this?" I honestly replied, "No, but it's happening, and we couldn't be happier!" Richard's father just got angry and declared that he wasn't raising this one. His reaction was so shocking and hurtful. What kind of person could say such a thing? Richard's parents were already raising their daughter's child and were expecting to have to raise her second child which would soon be born. I found Richard later on crying on the patio and drowning his sorrows in beer.

Next day at work, I told my friend Liz the good news and discussed with her how I could tell the broker, Mr. Rule. I had grown close to Liz and truly wanted to stay in the company. I went into the broker's office in tears, not knowing what to expect. Mr. Rule comforted me by saying, "Angel, honey, that is great! If you're happy, I'm happy!" He asked me if I were sure I could keep up the pace of this job and be a new mom. I assured him that I could, and I was ready to work even harder if needed. I felt so light and free after discovering I could keep my job.

I had morning sickness like clockwork at 1:30 a.m. every morning just as Richard got up for work, but I was ready to endure anything for my little blessing. Realizing I didn't know what else I had to endure, I made my first baby purchase, a book called *What to Expect When You're Expecting* by Heidi Murkoff. My workload kept me going until late in the evening with Richard already in bed. We usually spent time together on the weekends. We had a long talk about our new family and my concerns about his lifestyle.

The drinking had decreased, and I began to have hope that he had realized that there was more to life than partying. I believed in this motto: Life is new everyday with another opportunity to let go of the past, and let God make you new. Jezebel was in and out of our lives as she and Richard still argued about Teddy. I never understood what this argument involving Teddy was about but it would get heated quickly.

I was not the only one pregnant at home. Blondie was expecting puppies. Our neighbor's Doberman had been visiting her in our backyard. The neighbors, a gay couple, agreed to help us with the vet bill as Blondie was considered high-risk too. We began to develop a relationship with them through the dog connection. We even ended up taking a trip together to a chalet and were snowed in there. At one point, I woke up to find all three of the men together, drunk and in the hot tub. This didn't concern me at the time as the other two were a couple. I just saw it as another embarrassing drunk moment.

Into my second trimester, the morning sickness stopped and the cravings started. My main crave was onions with ice cream holding a close second. I began packing on the pounds. I tried to wear larger shirts and elastic pants to save money on maternity clothes. The weight gain didn't bother me as I loved knowing that the baby was growing inside of me.

Life was getting more stressful at home. I tried to keep stress levels down by zoning out of heated arguments, still hoping that things would change with the arrival of the baby. The drinking had increased again, and the times of intimacy decreased even more. Richard did not want to touch me in my condition. Oh, how I longed for a lasting hug or special kiss, some form of meaningful affection. Nevertheless, I was so full of joy thinking of our new little one and the upcoming gender appointment. I was hoping to talk Richard into going to this appointment with me as I had gone alone to all the others. I couldn't wait to feel the baby moving soon. I imagined my child to be loving, calm, and gentle as that is what had come to my heart. Would it be a boy or a girl? Richard told me that he felt the baby we lost was a boy. He usually talked about this while he was drunk. I didn't care what sex the baby was so long as it was healthy and happy. Whatever God blessed us with was fine with me. There was one trait that I hoped skipped our baby, though. All the girls on Richard's side had red hair.

Richard had to work late on the day of the appointment, so I went alone. I just knew that today was the day I would learn if I was carrying a boy or girl. I had prayerfully asked God to let us find out today, as the last time the sex was unclear. During the ultrasound, I could see the baby was developing well and I began to cry tears of joy. The baby seemed to have no damage or problems from the medicine or smoking. The technician said, "She looks great." She? Did I hear her right? Soon Dr. Howdy confirmed that we were having a baby girl! I just knew that Richard would be as excited as I was. I was also ready to start on my Winnie-the-Pooh nursery décor. My mom is artistic and crafty, and she had been working on something special for the baby's room.

On the way home, I remembered many of my own childhood experiences that I wanted to share with my daughter. Even though I was told I might not be able to have children, I saved many toys and dolls just in case. I couldn't give up hope that God had other plans for me. I had always loved children, and they had always loved me. I knew how to love, care for, and spoil children after helping to raise my nephew. I was ready to love and spoil my own!

Next, I began to think of names. It was funny how my mom picked out a girl name as soon as I told her the news. She wanted a granddaughter this time as she already had a grandson. Richard and I had discussed names before, but he wanted to wait until we knew the gender. I was on cloud nine riding home to talk to him. Normally, I would never wake him up after he had gone to bed, but I just couldn't wait. He awoke as I sat down beside him; he asked about the appointment. I burst into tears of joy as I shared everything with him. I even had an ultrasound photo that showed all her newly developed features, but it was too dark in the room to see it. He hugged me and told me he was so glad that I woke him up with the news, but he was tired and wanted to talk more tomorrow.

Next, I began to call all our friends and family. My mom was the first to get a call as she was most involved and had become my best friend during this time. We laughed and cried together, and I hoped to be even half the mom to my daughter as she had been to me. I knew that I could thank her for who I was today. Even though we didn't see eye to eye in my teenage years, I could see now how much she loved me through it all. She made a pitch for her favorite name, Victoria, or Vickie for short. I called my grandparents next who were also full of joy. My grandmother and my mom had been two stable rocks of faith and love in my family. Their influence shaped my character greatly. Richard's parents shared in the good news with a little less excitement than the others, but still positively. I also called Liz who had become such a good friend to me. Her humor always offset any unstable emotions I might be having.

I spent the next few hours looking through my baby name book at all the meanings and origins of names. I couldn't sleep all night as I excitedly thought about talking over names with Richard and celebrating together. Unfortunately, as it turned out, the name celebration would have to wait. The ringing phone woke me the next morning with Richard's mom calling to get in touch with him. Richard's grandfather was sick and worsening. This saddened me as Richard's grandparents were the only source of love in his family. They had loved and supported us through everything. I knew this would be hard for Richard. I was able to get a message through to him at work. Richard came home so we could go see his grandfather together. Richard had a few beers before we left, so I drove as usual. I was used to driving to keep him from getting a DUI and losing his job.

His grandfather, who had been a big man, looked so small and helpless. Just about everyone from Richard's side of the family was at his grandparents' home with him, including his father who started an argument with Richard. Richard stormed out after the argument, and we headed back home for a night of drinking and rage. I usually left him alone during times like these to avoid verbal criticism and abuse.

I had scheduled a visit with the OB/GYN, Dr. Howdy, making sure Richard and I were there like Dr. Howdy requested. I made the appointment for Richard's day off, and he reluctantly went along. They were changing my medicine during the later stages of pregnancy and would need to watch me even closer. I also needed to have special tests run to make sure the baby did not have club feet or a cleft palate, as these were side effects of the previous medication. I began to cry as this was the first I was hearing about this. As fear welled up inside of me, I looked over at Richard who seemed to be filling with anger. The doctor scheduled a 3D ultrasound at the hospital and told us that we would have to pay for the procedure as the insurance didn't cover it. I didn't care about the cost; I just wanted a happy, healthy baby. We rode in silence to the ultrasound. I felt faint as I was in shock and disbelief while Richard continued to look angrier. The test was quick, and I began to pray to God on behalf of my baby girl knowing He had never forsaken me in my time of need. I felt His peace and comfort coming over me as we waited for the results.

The radiologist called us into a private room and told us there were no signs of club feet or cleft palate. He also confirmed the baby was a girl. He concluded by saying he would send the scans to my doctor. I took a deep breath of relief and thanked God for answering my prayer. On the way home, Richard remained angry and told me that I should have had an abortion. I had been too shocked to cry until now, but after hearing this, the tears began to flow out of hurt and rejection. I blew up at Richard's response with language and anger that would make a sailor blush. At a time when I should have been rejoicing with the good news, I felt like a mama bear protecting her cub. I needed my husband's support right now, not blame and offense. Like other times, I went home and cried myself to sleep.

Richard apologized later and told me that he was scared and reacted wrongly. I was thankful for the apology and felt that God was restoring things between us. The week went by slowly before my next appointment. I was beginning to trust God more with the baby and Richard. I felt that God was giving me signs that He was in control. There was a supernatural light in the parking garage as I went to my appointment. I was even able to comfort a lady sitting near me in the lobby who was worried about her own scans. I reassured her and told her I would pray for her. Suddenly, I saw Richard coming down the hallway to meet me, saying, "Angel, I made it." It was hard for him to get off work, so I was surprised and pleased. I knew all these signs were confirmation of God's favor. Dr. Howdy confirmed to us that the tests looked good, and I had one more test in the office. I was so thankful for this wonderful day! I sure needed it!

I was at work when someone called to let me know the last test results were normal. I couldn't wait to tell Richard the news! He wasn't home when I got there, so I called his workplace and was told he had left earlier than normal. I waited for several hours and even called around looking for him. He finally called drunk from the bar to have me pick him up. He passed out when we got home. I found a phone number with the name "Jack" in his pocket as I was doing his laundry. I saved it for him on the counter figuring it was work related. He had a bad hangover the next morning. I noticed the phone number in the trash. He apologized for the previous day's events, telling me how stressed he had been and how he had needed a few drinks to relax. He didn't mean for it to go that far. I asked if he remembered me telling him about the test results, and he said it was great news.

About this same time, my doctor changed my seizure medication again to what was supposed to be an even safer drug. I was now in my sixth month of pregnancy and outgrowing everything. My onion cravings were getting worse, and I ate them with everything. I was having trouble finding shoes to fit my very swollen feet. My doctor told me to be watchful for preeclampsia, which was a concern to him. My blood sugar and blood pressure were closely monitored.

One morning I awoke to find increased swelling all over and blotching on my skin. I called the doctor and the nurse told me to come in immediately. I couldn't find anyone to drive me so I drove myself, crying and fearful all the way. They sent me straight over to the hospital, so I called my mom, Richard's mom, and Richard's work on the way. I was admitted to ICU for careful observation. Dr. Howdy looked worried; but, as always, he kept reassuring me that everything would be fine. I reminded myself how blessed I was to have him all these years. The nurses were watching me and the baby closely with many wires and instruments. They told me that I had an allergic reaction to the new medication. The baby was also reacting to it. I also had toxemia. I knew there was nothing else to do but trust God. Dr. Howdy told me that it was important for me to rest and be calm as both the baby and I were in critical condition and stress could make it worse. My parents and Richard came in at visiting hours. I could tell Richard had been crying. It was hard waiting to see them in between visits, but I knew that my baby and I were not alone. God was there as always, comforting me. I began to rub my belly and talk to the baby, telling her that God had a special plan for her life. I knew this was true as she was already a miracle in so many ways. I spoke Jeremiah 29:11 over her, one of my favorite Bible verses:

"For I know the plans I have for you," declares the Lord, "plans to prosper you and not to harm you, plans to give you hope and a future."

Then I felt her move. I had not been able to feel her move since waking that morning. A monitor went off, and the nurse ran in to check. She left smiling to tell the doctor the good news. I knew that God was agreeing with the verse. He had plans for this baby!

I began to work half-days and tried to be off my feet as much as possible. I continued to get the nursery ready for the baby, and we called Richard's grandfather frequently as he was doing worse. Richard continued to drink more often and keep distant. He had stopped talking to his family since my time in the hospital. He was angry that I had called them for help and they were too busy to take me to the hospital. Then they didn't come when I was in ICU. His grandfather died the next month, and the funeral was filled with drama as usual.

Over the next four weeks, the baby's movements began to slow, and I was told to keep a movement log. One night, I called the emergency number as she hadn't moved at all for many hours. My doctor was on vacation but had me rush to the hospital to be checked by his partner. The baby's heartbeat was low, and she wasn't moving much. They told me that she was stressed, and they needed to induce labor for the birth. I told them I would only let my doctor deliver her, so they called him, and he came. My parents came to the hospital, and Richard called in to work.

Everything seemed so chaotic, and the birth was not progressing. After 26 hours, Dr. Howdy decided to do a C-section. I began to cry as I had heard that I wouldn't be able to hold her or care for her if I had a C-section. I was determined to have her normally and talked the nurses into helping me. I summoned all my strength to push, and they called Dr. Howdy when her head was crowning. He came in very concerned but prepared for the delivery. When she was born, she gave just a little whimper instead of a loud cry. The room fell quiet and now everyone seemed concerned. She had some breathing issues at first and was put on oxygen. She also had some muscle weakness in her shoulder and arm. Her face was swollen and her head pointed like a cone. In all of it, I knew God would take care of her.

My baby girl was finally here in my arms! I just cried with joy looking at her. She weighed 8 pounds and 9 ounces. I counted ten fingers and ten toes. My mom was rubbing her head and shaping it saying her "little doll" would be just fine. The baby didn't want to nurse, so we bottle-fed her. I fell asleep with exhaustion as I thanked God for this miracle. I never knew I could love someone so much! I promised her that I would do everything in my power to protect her from hurt or harm. I also knew that we had protection from above.

Chapter 4:

OUR FIRST BLESSING

After several days in the hospital, the time had come to take our little Victoria home. My body still looked six months pregnant even though Victoria was four weeks premature, and I was dealing with the aftereffects of toxemia, but nothing could quench the unconditional love I had for this helpless little newborn. Joy filled my heart every time I held her and felt her snuggling up to me. Words couldn't describe the love I felt for her. I didn't want to put her down. I loved to study her face with perfect little lips and nose and eyelashes. Her beautiful dark eyes seemed to stare into my very soul. Her rosy pink skin and chubby cheeks framed a little face with mixed features of mine and Richard's. What a perfect combination! She seemed absolutely perfect inside and out. I felt so full of peace and contentment and purpose.

Victoria was a bit swollen at first and wouldn't fit into some of the "preemie" clothes at 8 pounds 9 ounces. We couldn't even button the back of her "coming home" dress for the hospital pictures. By the time we were home, she had already overcome the weakness in her shoulder and the breathing issues she had at birth. I was constantly filled with thankfulness and gratitude to God who had given me a perfect baby girl in spite of what had been expected. I knew she was a miracle! I knew that she was my "little piece of heaven" that would make up for all the pain I had endured.

I had heard that being a mother came with its own rewards and heartaches; nevertheless, I loved it! It was utter happiness to me! Of course, life was different at home as I adjusted to a new routine of feeding and changing the baby every two hours. I wasn't normally a napper, so I would go until my body just shut down from exhaustion. The days seemed to fly by as my four weeks of maternity leave were almost over. Work and financial need were pressing on me. I found a part-time sitter named Kay who was thrilled to watch Victoria while I went back to work. Her own children and grandchildren were grown. Richard would stay with the baby on his day off, and I would cover the evenings and weekends. Each night I cherished coming home to spend time with Victoria. She was changing so quickly!

In my heart, I truly wished I could stay home with Victoria, but Richard expected me to work if he worked. I knew this before we were married. He would spend his days with Victoria watching TV with her lying on his chest. Jezebel wasn't part of our lives during this time because of an argument. This meant more attention from Richard for the baby and me. It also meant less drinking and drama. Even after my body healed, Richard didn't seem interested in sex. He was afraid I might get pregnant again too soon like his mother did. My family visited often, but Richard's family visited only rarely.

When I received news that my mom had breast cancer, I was distressed to think that Victoria might grow up without her Nana. I decided to visit them as much as possible and pray that Victoria would have the blessing of grandparents like I did.

As the months passed, Victoria began eating and sleeping regularly. Richard's lifestyle was calmer, and he seemed more pleasant and less irritable. Our home seemed filled with peace and love just like I had hoped and prayed for over the years. I felt that God was using Victoria to make a difference in our lives already. I hoped that one day she would make a difference in the world. We eventually enrolled her in a full-time day care. Richard would pick her up and make dinner for us each day. I spent all the time I could with her in the evenings as I worked long hours all week. We tried to find time to spend as a family on the weekends, enjoying many firsts together—first tooth; first words; first time rolling, sitting, and crawling; and of course, first steps. Victoria was already becoming a toddler!

Every day was brighter with our little angel! Love and laughter filled every minute. Victoria had also taken a special love of animals. She wanted to pet every cat or dog we saw and fell in love with the farm animals at my grandparents' home. Once she gave her pacifier to a little calf, but then regretfully wanted it back after many sleepless nights. Victoria also loved people. She had such a giving, loving personality for such a little one.

We had a big birthday celebration in our backyard when Victoria turned one. Just about all our friends and family came, including those from other states. Jezebel also came back into our lives at the party, and the drinking started again. That night, Richard wanted to be intimate after having several beers. I wasn't sure why but decided to enjoy it as I wasn't sure how long it would be before he would feel that way again. I still hoped that Richard would one day give his life to God, and our lives would change for the better.

Life flew by as we watched Victoria changing and growing. She began talking in full sentences and coloring and watching princess movies. We had to take her crib out of her room and give her a bed when she began climbing out of it. We spent the weekends visiting some of Richard's family, although his relationship with his father had been strained after they had words again. Some of the change was not for the better. After such a long time of joy, it seemed that Richard and I were growing apart again. Remembering my commitment, I was determined to hold onto our marriage even though it seemed that there was only one unraveled thread holding us together.

Chapter 5:

LEAVING ISN'T ALWAYS EASY

I began taking much more responsibility with Victoria as Richard's drinking began to increase. Although I loved all my time with her, the drinking seemed like a dark cloud hanging over us with no hope of the sun shining again. We made an appointment with a professional marriage counselor who suggested that we get away together, just the two of us. He felt that all the stress of a new baby, my mother's sickness, and Richard's family issues was affecting our relationship. Richard's Aunt Dolly volunteered to keep Victoria for us as my mom was undergoing radiation treatments. I kept much of the circumstances of our lives from my mom as she was stressed enough with her health. I

was also too ashamed and prideful to admit our problems to anyone. Aunt Dolly tried to give me advice on
my marriage as she had dealt with the problem of an
alcoholic husband while being the main breadwinner
for the family and raising kids that were now adults.
She was a very strong woman, but I could sense that
all the pain and trauma had taken a toll on her.

Richard and I decided to book an all-inclusive trip
to Mexico. I was excited but torn about leaving our
one-and-a-half-year-old daughter behind. I kept myself busy with all the preparations so I wouldn't worry.
I was determined for this trip to be nothing but a great
memory. At the resort, the rooms were rather dark
and dingy and smelled of mold. But I had booked several activities to get us out and about, which I hoped
would brighten the atmosphere. One thing I wasn't
counting on was that "all-inclusive" included "all the
alcohol you could drink" as well. We spent the first
morning by the pool near the beach with Richard
spending most of his time at the pool bar. As he took
a nap after too much to drink, I read in the hammock
on the beach. That night I booked a dinner with a
fire dance and show. Richard wasn't feeling well and
decided to go back to the room during the show. He
told me to stay and enjoy it, that he would be fine. I
decide to go and check on him during the intermis-
sion as, once again, he had consumed much alcohol.

I was surprised when I couldn't find him in the room. It had been over an hour since he left, and our room was just a 10-minute walk from the dinner location. I questioned the front desk employee who had not seen him go through. I retraced my steps back and forth wondering if he had passed out somewhere. Finally, the man at the front desk told me that he saw him go through to the room. Relieved, I ran there to find him completely naked and passed out on the bed. So many questions were going through my mind about where he had been and with whom. I had heard horror stories of people being drugged in foreign countries and horrible things happening. I would need to wait until morning to find out the truth.

I awoke at 8 a.m. and Richard was not there. I quickly dressed and went downstairs to find him on the veranda drinking coffee. He asked about the show and claimed that he went straight back to the room when he left. I was very heated and confused over this, but I didn't want to start an argument on our second day. I was angry at myself for the high expectations I had made which were being crushed again. We spent another day out at the pool which was a copy of the day before. I did go and check on Richard this time to make sure he was really in the room taking a nap. Then I sat by the beach trying to refocus my mind and thoughts.

That night I had scheduled a dinner cruise for us. We met another couple at our table, and both men began to overdrink. The other man spent the trip vomiting over the railing, and Richard became "the life of the party" as usual. Two women were up on chairs pouring tequila and vodka into the mouths of anyone who ran under. Richard ran through multiple times, drawing attention to himself. What kind of party ship did I book? This was not what I had expected. Richard came over and started groping on me and trying to remove my shirt. I was so embarrassed and ashamed of how he was acting. I couldn't wait for the ride to be over! I slept in the extra bed that night. There had been no romantic intimacy so far.

Richard woke me the next morning after going down for coffee. He acted as if everything was grand, talking about the crazy night and having too much to drink. After seeing my face, he gave me the usual lecture about being a stick-in-the-mud and letting my bun down, which infuriated me. I got dressed and went down for breakfast, missing my daughter and wanting to leave her dad. I just felt so overwhelmed and tired of it all. I felt uncomfortable leaving Victoria alone with him because of the drinking. I was constantly wondering who she might be around or if he was drunk or passed out. My head hurt so bad from holding back tears that I felt a migraine or seizure might be coming on.

There was no sign of Richard when I went back to the room, so I went down to the beach to clear my thoughts. As my headache worsened, I went back to the room again and had a light seizure. I fell asleep and awoke to a quiet room shortly after lunchtime. During my shower, I could hear Richard come into the room clearly drunk and asking where I had been. He said he had been at the pool bar all morning waiting on me. Then he began yelling for me to come to the bed; he was waiting on me. By the time I finished showering and fixing my hair, he was passed out. I knew I needed to stay calm, so I went down to a shaded hut and read for four hours while listening to the ocean waves.

Upon returning, I found Richard drinking coffee on the balcony and wanting to talk. He said he could explain and wanted to go to dinner later. He gave a lengthy, vague excuse as my mind wandered. At dinner, he only had a beer and actually started opening up about having a hard time dealing with disturbing memories that had been coming to him after moving into his childhood home and raising his daughter there. My heart began to soften as he began to cry. I suggested he share these things with the therapist. I also offered to move to a new residence if he thought another home would be a good idea. He agreed that might help, and I began to let hope grow again, thinking of a new start and maybe even going back to church together. We made love that night, and it seemed a turn for the better. Richard still drank the rest of the trip, but we had no more episodes and he seemed more affectionate to me. We ended up buying a time-share for a newer condo nearby, and the remainder of the trip seemed so much lighter and enjoyable.

Overjoyed to be back with Victoria, I began preparing to sell our home. Besides moving, we were busy with the holidays. Richard's drinking slowed, and he was going to the therapist and to church occasionally. He seemed more content as I prayed for God to give him peace. We settled into a routine again as a family. After we moved, we ended up with great new neighbors who had children Victoria's age. I began working long hours again but took Victoria to work with me on Saturdays. We spent the weekend making family visits. My mom was undergoing radiation again with chemo following. I would usually cry after my visits with her, feeling numb and powerless; but she never gave in to the victim mentality, glorifying God through it all.

It seemed our life was getting back on track. One weekend, at a special dinner, Richard brought up the idea of having another child. The thought of a sibling for Victoria thrilled me. We discussed the pros and cons of my health issues and, by the end of the dinner, we agreed to start trying. My doctor gave me the green light with some precautions and recommendations. Victoria was not on board with a new baby at first but soon came around, making sure that she would always be her daddy's little princess.

We planned another trip to Mexico with Mary and Edward, an older couple we loved. We hoped for some intimate time together on this trip as our lives had been so busy lately. I did feel sick before the trip, but the pregnancy test was negative. The first few days were wonderful, but then Richard began binge drinking and felt bad the rest of the trip. Most of our friends didn't know about Richard's secret battle with alcoholism, but Mary and Edward became concerned after seeing it firsthand. I was having second thoughts on another baby. I asked Richard to see the therapist again, and he reluctantly agreed.

The sick feeling returned when I started back to work, so I took another pregnancy test that was positive. Richard and I were both ecstatic but waited on a confirmatory test from the doctor before spreading the good news. First, we told Victoria at a special dinner. She clapped her hands and was so happy for a baby brother or sister. That evening, we made several other phone calls. After putting Victoria to bed, I finally sat down with tears of joy to ponder this second blessing from God. Having Victoria had brought more happiness and joy to my life than I could have ever imagined. I could not even think of life without her. Now, I would get to enjoy that all over again. Children were indeed the greatest reward outside of salvation.

The second pregnancy presented totally different than the first. I already looked pregnant at three months, but with far fewer seizures and no medication changes. The doctor would again watch me and the baby closely. My mom came over as much as possible during my pregnancy. Victoria loved her Nana, and they had a special bond. She told everyone about her "sester" even though we hadn't yet determined the baby's gender. When I would laugh and say, "What about a brother?" she just yelled "No, no, no … a sester!" every time.

I began to feel tired by mid-afternoon daily, and I stopped going to church as much because of the fatigue. It was very important for me to raise my children in church, so I planned to get back as soon as possible. The baby was very active compared to Victoria and seemed to be setting lower. This made me think it could be a boy. I started having some swelling and blood pressure increase early in the fourth month. The doctor had me take some time off work to rest and visit him every two weeks.

I had hoped Richard would accompany me to the gender reveal visit, but he didn't have any time off from work. Victoria was telling her day care that she was getting her "sester" this week. We had already chosen a new Winnie-the-Pooh pattern for the baby that would work for either sex. During the ultrasound, the baby was moving so much that it took extra time to get a good look. Finally, the technician announced that it was a girl! I couldn't wait to tell Victoria that her prayers had been answered. She was laughing in the car seat and saying, "I have a sester!" I ran to tell Richard the news when he came home from work. It was such a special family dinner that night!

A few weeks later, I nearly fainted at work and had to be taken to the hospital. My blood pressure was very high and the swelling was very concerning to all. I began prayer for my sweet baby as it was way too early for her to be born. I asked Richard to pray with me when he arrived. I was sent home on bed rest for a month. My clients were very understanding, and Liz handled everything in the office for me as I could only do computer work and phone calls at home. I couldn't pick up Victoria or play on the floor with her. We adjusted by moving our playtime to the couch. She liked rubbing my belly and feeling the baby kick.

As Father's Day approached during my sixth month of pregnancy, I got permission from the doctor to have a picnic in the mountains with Richard and Victoria. I planned to get a bucket of chicken with drinks in the cooler, and Victoria made Richard a special card. Victoria spent some special time with her daddy and the dog the night before and got especially dirty and smelly. While bathing her, I felt a pain in the lower abdomen but was otherwise okay. Richard and I agreed upon the baby's name that night. She would be named after our two grandmothers, Libby Grace.

During the night, I awoke with pains which would come and go. I was uncomfortably large by now, actually the same size I was when Victoria was born. I assumed the pain was from overdoing it the day before, so I checked on Victoria and went back to bed. The next morning, I had an upset stomach and some more pain while getting in the truck. Richard decided we should stop at the hospital on the way to the picnic just to get checked. On the way to the hospital, we told Victoria that we had decided on Libby Grace for the baby's name. She laughed and said, "No, she's my sester!"

Chapter 6:

OUR SECOND BLESSING

Richard dropped me off at the obstetrician area of the hospital so I could get a quick check while he and Victoria waited in the truck. I felt a bit of urine come out as I left the truck. When I told the nurse inside, she quickly got me a wheelchair and rushed me into a room as she yelled instructions to other nursing staff. I told her that Richard and Victoria were out in the truck, and she informed me that we would need to get someone to come for Victoria and bring Richard inside. I tried to remain calm so my blood pressure wouldn't go up, but I was quickly getting scared. The test strip showed that the liquid was amniotic fluid and not urine. My baby was only six months along and didn't need to be born so prematurely. Her heart and lungs were still developing.

Dr. Howdy was on the way, along with my parents and Aunt Dolly to pick up Victoria. I was crying and praying again. I knew that Libby Grace was a blessing from God, and He was the one who could help us. My doctor came in to examine me about the same time Richard came in. He told us that our little girl would be born soon. She still had plenty of amniotic fluid around her, so he wanted to wait several hours for my blood pressure to go down. He would contact the emergency team and ICU care unit at the Children's Hospital where she would likely be transferred for special care after birth. My job was to try to calm down. That was not an easy job!

Richard broke the silence in the room by saying, "This little girl looks like she will be here on Father's Day." Thinking about what a daddy's girl Victoria was, I announced that I preferred to wait until tomorrow so she could be devoted to me as well. He laughed and said that it looked like she had made a decision to come no matter what! It felt so good to laugh and be lighthearted!

Richard went out to smoke when the nurse came in. I recognized her as one of the nurses that helped when Victoria was born. She definitely remembered the "talking to" she got from the doctor after Victoria was born vaginally rather than by C-section. We both laughed, and then I explained to her how scared I was for this baby to be born so early. She said, "Now, let's just pray about this. I am sure the good Lord will see you through this. After all, He has been with you this far, right?" At that moment, I was calmed by the memories of all that God had done for me. I thanked Him for giving me these two children when I had been told that I wouldn't have any. She prayed such a strong prayer that I was immediately comforted.

It was after midnight when I was awakened by extreme pain and more fluid. The doctor told me that they would prep the OR and we would have a baby within the hour. Richard kissed my forehead as they took me back to surgery. He smiled and said, "I'll be right there with you. I love you." I had turned it all over to God with the faith of a mustard seed. I had also decided to have my tubes tied while in surgery because of all the medical issues. As I was being prepped in the OR, Richard appeared by my side all suited up in a surgical cap and gown with mask and gloves. He said, "It's gonna be okay, Angel." He wiped a tear from my cheek and, at that moment, I knew why I had stayed with him.

A few moments later, the doctor laid on my chest a tiny, unmoving baby covered in dark, fine hair all over her body. She had a head full of black hair and ten fingers and toes. Then our Libby Grace was immediately taken away and put in a nearby incubator. She would be transferred to the Children's Hospital neonatal ICU and needed Richard to accompany her. My mom would stay with me for now. I began to cry and feel sick to my stomach with the room spinning, so the nurse gave me something through the IV and I was out.

I woke up crying out for my baby girl Libby with excruciating pain ripping through my body. My tired-looking mom rushed to my side to take my hand and remind me that she was here and so was God. She reminded me that His will for us is good. She tried to calm me down since my emotional state was causing my blood pressure to climb, making my monitors sound. The nurse also tried to calm me down, but so many thoughts were running through my mind. My heartache was so severe thinking of my Victoria confused without her mommy and my Libby Grace alone in a "box" going through God knows what! Mom soothed me, reminding me that Libby was in good hands at the Children's Hospital, but I just wanted to hold my baby and see her for myself. She was so small and still and lifeless when I saw her. The nurse said that a visit could probably be arranged, but I needed to be able to get up and walk to the bathroom without assistance. I knew that I could do anything to see my Libby.

When my blood pressure lowered after some rest, the nurse returned to help me to the restroom. After that painful experience, my mom held me up while they changed my bedding. My fears about Libby not coming home were overwhelming. Mom on occasion wiped my tears and said, "Angel, we aren't going to talk or think that way. We're going to pray together right now. God has a purpose for this little one, and He is the one who can heal her and deliver her back to us healthy and whole. She will come home to us." I immediately felt the need to kneel down, pain and all. Mom helped me to the floor, and we prayed together as the floor was covered in my tears. I pleaded with God, asking Him to show mercy to this baby girl. I promised to give her to Him from that day forward and trust her life to His grace.

When they got me back into the bed and gave me something for pain, I felt a seizure coming on. Several hours later, I came to and my mom gave me an update on Libby. She was on a ventilator with 100 percent oxygen and was getting surfactant shots for her lung development. I felt much more peaceful, as even the doctor could tell. He told me he would give me a two-hour pass to see Libby if I got plenty of rest and did well overnight. I tried to rest, though thoughts of my girls still filled my mind. I found out Victoria was with Richard's parents who didn't babysit her often. My heart was aching for her alone and confused. I just wanted to hold her and tell her everything would be fine. I was thinking of Richard, worried and alone with Libby Grace. I wanted to put my arms around him and tell him the same thing.

When I awoke, Mom and Richard were by my side. I sat up suddenly fearing that something had happened to Libby. Richard smiled and leaned over to kiss me saying that she was the same, but I had given everyone a big scare. I had another seizure, so they called in my neurosurgeon. He felt like the pain level and weakness was lowering my threshold levels. I promised to do my best to rest and be peaceful if I could just see my girls. My doctor reluctantly said he would still give me the two-hour pass and allow Victoria in for a brief visit tomorrow. The nurses started me on a breast pump so Libby could have the extra nutrients from breast milk. It was so important for "preemies," as it was more easily digestible. I hesitantly asked my doctor if I had done anything to cause the premature birth. He chuckled and said, "She broke your water because she was ready to be born." That gave me the peace I needed.

I awoke the next morning in pain but did not ask for medication in fear that it might delay my visit with my girls. Mom was out for her radiation treatment but came back as I was attempting to adjust myself in the bed. The nurses took me to the bathroom and informed me that the doctor wanted me to get up and sit in the chair for short periods of time before leaving. I knew this was in preparation for the car ride to see Libby. This seemed like the longest 24 hours of my life! I started shaking and felt tears of fear forming as I had thoughts again that Libby would not come home. My mom looked me in the eyes and said, "Let's get down right here and give this baby and all her future to the Lord." We got back on our knees on the floor and did just that. While we were praying, I felt a hand on my shoulder that seemed to lift off the burden of fear. I knew my mom's hands were holding mine, so I determined it must have been God taking that from me. I instantly felt relief and felt the fear leave my heart and mind. I easily got up from the floor and stored this miracle away to tell my baby girl someday.

Doctor Howdy had signed the paperwork for me to see Libby from 2 to 4 p.m. after hearing how well I had done that morning. Before we left, I had my visit from Victoria. Richard had picked her up at Aunt Dolly's home and brought her to see me. Mom grabbed Victoria as she launched herself at me. Mom sat her on the bed where she could wrap her arms around me in a special hug. Victoria was full of joy and laughter and not short on conversation as she told me all the events of the last day. She kept gently touching my face to keep my attention focused on her stories. She finally asked about baby Libby Grace. I explained that nurses were taking care of her at another hospital and that we would bring her home when she was better.

After that special visit, Mom and I drove to the Children's Hospital. When we arrived at the ICU, I was excited to think I was about to see Libby Grace for the second time. Mom and I had to get our gowns and gear on before entering the nursery full of incubators. Mom gave me a hug to quiet my shakiness as we made our way to Libby's incubator. Tiny could not even describe the baby I saw there, with tubes coming and going from every direction. A baby boy next to her was even smaller in size. I just wanted to pick Libby Grace up and hold her and tell her that Mommy was here. To my surprise, the nurses took us back into a special room to let us hold and cuddle her. They said they had been telling her all morning that Mommy and Nana were coming to visit today.

I cried as Libby tried to open her eyes when she heard my voice. I knew that God was answering my prayers. I knew in my heart that I would see her come home with me one day soon. The hours went by quickly as I held and talked to her. I was completely exhausted, but leaving was so hard as I kissed her little forehead and told her Mommy would be back soon. I broke down in the car, feeling like I was abandoning her. When we returned to the hospital, they fussed at me for staying longer than was acceptable. My mom and I both fell asleep exhausted but hopeful that we would see Libby again the next day.

The nurse helped me with a shower the next morning, and I found out the doctor was releasing me after lunch! I was so excited knowing that I would be able to see Richard, Victoria, and Libby now that I could go home. I promised Dr. Howdy that I would rest and told my mom the good news when she returned from her treatment. The house was quiet when we got there as both Richard and Victoria were napping. Mom and I laid down for naps as well. I woke to some small fingers rubbing my face ever so gently. I let Victoria lie beside me on the couch, and we hugged each other for quite a while. She asked about baby Libby, and I told her that she would come home soon.

I took some pain medication before we went to see Libby that afternoon. When we arrived at the ICU, we had to wait a bit before going in. The little boy I had seen in the incubator beside Libby had passed away, and there were procedures going on in the nursery at the moment. I was so shaken by this that I had to sit down. I refused to let fear back in by thinking that one day this same thing could happen to us. I had to trust

God that He was healing and forming her little body even now. The nurse allowed me to go in and pump some breast milk, and then it was our turn to see our precious baby. She seemed more alert today, and the nurse told us they were not sedating her as much so she would learn to breathe on her own. Suddenly it was time to leave. Richard and I didn't speak about the baby boy on the way home. Neither of us could bear it. Nana and Victoria were settled in on the couch watching a princess movie when we returned.

Week after week, this became our normal routine. Victoria began having some urinary accidents, and I was having more seizures than normal. Dr. Rye, my neurologist, wanted to wait until I was finished pumping breast milk before he increased any of my medication. Libby was improving so much. She was off the ventilator and breathing on her own. She would probably be discharged sooner than expected. They warned us early on that there were possible side effects from prolonged oxygen and some other drugs used to keep her alive as a "preemie." I still decided to trust that God would make her whole. She was still small, three pounds lighter than Victoria was when she was born. Her little eyes seemed to look for us as we talked to her. Her little fingers wrapped around ours and her little toes wiggled in excitement. She was still a wiggler like she was when I carried her inside.

I took pictures of Libby for Victoria when we visited, and she carried them with her to show everyone.

We were back to an almost normal routine at home with work and day care. Mom went back home as she had completed her treatments. Richard had been doing some landscaping in the yard, and we still had our late afternoon Libby visits. During the days leading up to her homecoming, we had to learn important information about her health and care. We needed to be cautious not to bring home any respiratory viruses to our "preemie" which could potentially be dangerous to her. The doctors told us that she could be more susceptible to respiratory illness until she was three or four years old. When she came home, one of us would need to sleep in the room with her. She would need to be fed every two hours and would be wearing a heart monitor. None of this information hindered our excitement. I awoke at 6 a.m. the morning we were scheduled to go pick up Libby. After two months we were so ready to bring our new addition home!

Chapter 7:

NEW HOPE DAWNS

Tears of joy and gratefulness streamed down my face as we brought Libby home. We had a hard first year with RSV (respiratory syncytial virus) and some other setbacks, yet we still felt blessed with our two beautiful, miracle girls. Victoria was madly in love with her baby sister, and Libby couldn't take her eyes off Victoria. The two developed such a close bond. Almost four years old, Victoria was a big help with Libby and our new routine. Her love and kindness overflowed to her little sister. She also loved her new dog Woody. We lost Blondie after some health complications. I loved listening to Victoria describe God's great, big world from her child's point of view. It almost made me want to be a child again myself. I began taking the girls to church when it was safe for Libby to be around crowds.

Unfortunately, Richard began drinking again. I was drawn to him like a moth to a flame during the good times, but then he would pull back from me, leaving me feeling cold and alone. Whenever I tried to talk to him about his behavior when he was drinking, he would turn the tide and accuse me of being crazy, bipolar, erratic, or selfish. He felt that I was the one with all the issues and saw himself as the normal one. The vicious cycle was destroying me. He was living life as a big party with me on the sidelines feeling helpless to pull down the charade.

Now that I had two beautiful faces looking to me for guidance and protection, I started feeling that we deserved more. I would do all I could to give my girls the best life possible. I wasn't sure why God had not broken through to Richard. I had been praying for so long, knowing that He was the only one who could make a change. I decided to focus on the girls now. I also had to focus on another move. Richard felt uncomfortable with our neighbors. He felt like they were always watching him, and he had no privacy. He decided to move us into a new house that was surrounded by several acres of land. He seemed happier once we were settled in the new place, but the girls were left without neighborhood friends. They still had each other, though.

Libby could not attend day care, so she stayed with me. Richard had little time for anything besides work and keeping up the large yard. I was stretched very thin with working long hours, taking Victoria to day care and Libby to work with me, raising two girls, and trying to visit my mom in a hospital four hours away. Mom had had a bone marrow transplant, so I was driving at night to be with her as much as possible. Aunt Dolly was my backup sitter allowing me to make the trips late evenings to see my mom when needed. She would keep both Victoria and Libby for me on days she was off work. After two weeks in the hospital, Mom contracted a rare bacterial infection. Because her body was so weak from the cancer and transplant drugs, she finally couldn't fight anymore. At 26 years old, I lost my dearest and best friend. Our relationship had deepened so much after my children came. I was devastated.

I began grief counseling but felt very little love and support from Richard. Because he had never been close to his mother, he felt that I should just be able to move on. He said hurtful words to me when he had been drinking. My counselor felt like Richard should seek help, too, but he was in denial. Victoria was starting to act out at day care and pull back from my hugs.

She really missed her Nana. I told her Nana was in heaven. We read a book about it and talked about her often. The counselor told me not to worry as Victoria may be distancing herself in fear that she might lose others she loved.

One day, Victoria said that Daddy told her I loved Libby more. This was a big shock. I tried to explain to Victoria that I loved them both equally even though I spent more time with Libby to care for her. I tried to share with her that parents can love their children equally but show it in different ways. I knew that she was too little to grasp any of it. She declared that she was Daddy's only princess, and she loved him. This was so painful, but I reminded her again of my love even though she was Daddy's princess. Not sure how Richard could have told her these things, I just began to pray.

Victoria was an outside girl who loved basketball, bike rides, animals, and nature. Libby preferred to be inside watching TV or playing games. Although our girls were quite different, they had some similar characteristics. They were both loving and kindhearted. Neither of them liked injustice and were bold to stand up for anyone being treated unfairly. They were growing too fast, and I was so pleased with them. My life was always on the go with work, school, and activities. Richard liked to cook, so he usually cooked dinner for us when we got home. I tried to make sure that we had family dinner out at least twice a week to spend time together. Richard became the "fun dad" who was only there when he wanted to participate. Where school activities were concerned, he usually stayed in bed, and the girls would tell him about our adventures when we returned. He did love outdoor activities, though, like playing in the pool with the girls. Many times, he would sit with Victoria and just let her talk to him. I always admired him for that.

Over the months and years, each of our daughters made a special friend at school. These two best friends became like two more children to me. I often took them to work and other activities with us, and they stayed the night regularly. I hoped these four would be best friends for life. As the girls had to accompany me to work so much, we often took breaks at lunchtime to go to the park or go bowling. I never left the girls alone with Richard when their friends were over. I had become close to both the mothers, but they weren't aware of Richard's drinking problem. They just knew that he didn't want the responsibility to watch the kids, so the girls were always with me.

We tried to have a weekly routine for some stability at home. After weekday dinners we would get homework done and then have outside activities or indoor movies and games. Victoria was a bad loser and would usually quit if she thought she was losing. Before bed we had a bedtime story and prayer with a hug and a kiss each night. I spent time with Richard on his day off and Sundays after church. Our times of intimacy were few and far between, yet I remained loyal and devoted to him. It seemed that all our family time included alcohol when Richard was with us. I didn't want the girls to see this as normal life, so I tried to shelter them from it as much as possible. Still, from time to time, a confrontation flared up between me and Richard, with Richard telling the girls that I was overreacting and that I was a stick-in-the-mud that needed to let her bun down. All the secrecy was so exhausting. I felt like I had lost the battle long ago and was just on a merry-go-round, getting off and back on the same ride but going nowhere.

As Victoria entered her pre-teen years, she began to idolize her father and to back talk and disrespect me. She did everything she could to try to please him and get his approval. Both girls wanted Daddy's attention desperately but showed it in different ways. Richard seemed incapable of investing himself in any relationship, and it was creating a wedge between him and our girls. I knew their pain, and I hurt for them. Libby always seemed withdrawn from him as Richard had not taken as much time with her out of fear for her condition. She was becoming a loner and showing

some of the manipulative traits Richard used to protect herself from the heartache. I thought I was doing
the best thing by keeping our family together and
living a life of anxiety and excuses. I thought I could
keep everything going while sheltering the girls from
hurt and buffering the effects of an alcoholic father.
Maybe I had been deceived. It seemed there was no
way to keep them from eventually being hurt and feeling rejected. I was empty, tired, and exhausted, and I
just couldn't fight anymore.

Aunt Dolly invited me and the girls to go to church
with her in the hope that Richard might see his Uncle
Willis attending and come along. I had been consid-
ering a fresh start at a healthy church with a youth
group where my girls could grow and get more involved. Victoria had started an unhealthy relationship
with a woman mentor at our home church. I had been
watching her grow to resent me more and more while
trying to please this woman. I really loved my home
church, but I was beginning to see a need to make a
break from this woman's influence. I also felt myself
declining spiritually. I hadn't been spending much
time reading the Bible or worshiping God. I felt that
my prayers were accomplishing nothing. My hope
in God's ability to change Richard was waning after
14 years, and I even felt angry at Him. I felt ashamed
for being mad at God, and I felt guilty for making the

wrong choice of keeping our family together. I began to blame myself. I couldn't find peace or my faith. I couldn't see any freedom from the generational curse we lived under.

I tried to repent of my anger as we went to the new church that first Sunday morning. I chose to hope in a new beginning and a restoration of my relationship with God. The congregation was much smaller than at our old church, but Victoria found a little friend immediately. Libby was content to sit with me as always. I felt God speaking to me through the message that day. The tears flowed as I began to release all the fear and bitterness that had been kept in my heart. On the way home the girls asked why I was crying. I told them I was cleaning out my eyes and my soul. Once home, they ran out to the pool, where Richard had been drinking, and told him about the new church. They told him that I had cried. He looked at me and laughed and asked if that was true. I told him yes.

Later that evening when we were alone, he asked me what it was that made me cry. I told him that I had much to get off my chest. I asked him to go with us next week so he could hear for himself. He said that if he went to church again, the place would burn down. I disagreed with him and asked him to please think about it for the girls' sake. I heard Victoria asking him through the week, and to my surprise, he went to church with us the following weekend.

Richard began to attend church regularly, and my hope for our marriage began to rise. I gave my life to Jesus and was baptized at age seven, and both my girls had accepted salvation during the years at our old church. Richard told me that he was saved as a young boy during a camp meeting but never mentioned being baptized. I was hoping that now his relationship with God would begin to blossom and my long-time prayers would be answered. Although Richard was still drinking, we began to talk more, and our relationship began to improve. We discussed the services and what feelings they brought out. Libby had made a friend, so both girls were going to children's church now. Our entire family seemed to enjoy going to church together. Richard's Uncle Willis came over, and they would drink together and talk about God and even sing some hymns together. After a few months, the drinking began to slow again, and we started to go out on date nights again. I felt like I was seeing a glimpse of the man I fell in love with years ago. Everyone began to be happier and more content.

Three months later, an unexpected resurgence crashed our happy home. Thankfully, the girls weren't home at the time. Richard started drinking at an outdoor birthday party for my sister. The music was flowing throughout the property, and we had people sitting in the pavilion by the pool, guests inside the house, and guests in chairs around a fire pit with a large fire burning as it was early October. Richard ignored my pleas to stop drinking and was out of control. He was tipping chairs and inadvertently hurt my sister. He stood laughing at the fire like a devil as I was screaming over the loud music to try to get his attention. I tried to put my arms over his shoulders and around his neck, and he threw me off by raising his hands and hitting me on both sides of my face and head. My brother Al stepped in and punched him, knocking him out. I was shocked but knew that Al was defending me. People began to leave. Aunt Dolly and Uncle Willis went out to talk to Richard when they could sit him up. My sister told me that Richard needed help. I felt my new dreams and hopes were falling to the ground.

This event began the out-of-control spiral that we had experienced before. Richard explained away his black eye as the result of goofing off. He began drinking heavily and quit attending church. At this same time, my brother Al lost a five-year battle with cancer which added to the pain. I felt like the two people in the world I could depend on were gone. I knew that I couldn't lose Richard now, too.

Richard was angry with me and blamed me for the fight between him and Al. He was hurting because the friendship had not been repaired before Al passed away. He would usually bring it up when he was drunk. At one point, I took the girls and got in the car and told Richard we were leaving. This just made the girls mad at me. Richard hollered from the pool for them to get out of the car and stay home, that I was just being crazy. They did exactly that, not understanding my reason for wanting to leave him, as I had hidden so much from them over the years. An evil voice like the devil himself taunted me from Richard's mouth as I got out of the car to go inside with the girls. "See, Angel, they aren't ever leaving with you. They don't care about you. Just go cry in the house!" Then he called me several names as I went to bed to avoid him.

I decided to research functional alcoholism. Both sides of Richard's family were cursed with this problem. He also had many traumatic events in early childhood that added to his deep pain. I learned that I had become an enabler to him. The fact that he had become physically aggressive was something new. He had never before been physically abusive to me, and I had determined in my heart that I would not submit to that behavior. I knew that I couldn't do anything to change this, but my hope remained in God who could bring healing and freedom to him. I decided to get some godly counsel from my new pastor, even though I was afraid to let it all out.

I tried to talk to Richard the night before the appointment, but he just blamed me for everything, as usual. He even encouraged me to go to counseling, saying I was the one who needed help. I was haunted by thoughts of divorce, something I had rarely considered. I was shaking as I waited at the pastor's door. I found myself pouring out my entire life's story like I never had before. Everything I had hidden behind closed doors came rushing out like an endless fountain. God wanted me to let go of the built-up anger and resentment and to receive His peace. Even in the midst of all the emotions, I realized that I still loved Richard. I revealed to the pastor my fear of leaving the girls alone with him and how deceived they were about him. I told him about the revelation that I had been an enabler when I thought I was taking the best option by overlooking, concealing, and making excuses for Richard. I was living a life of lies. I didn't know who I was anymore. The last 15 years were spent fighting for our love, marriage, and family, but I was too defeated to continue the fight. Alcoholism was a terrible disease for which I didn't have the cure.

I had almost cried myself into a migraine and was mentally exhausted by the end of the meeting. The pastor told me that he had experience with addiction, and he agreed to talk to Richard. He asked me not to leave the marriage just yet as he felt that God could still heal and restore Richard and our family. We prayed together and asked God to release Richard from the addiction and lies and replace them with a heart for God and the purposes of God for his life, marriage, and family. We asked that our family could receive back all the enemy had stolen from us.

On the way home I felt some release, but still knew a big decision was coming up for me. I felt different than I had in the past, as if something had shifted. Victoria and her friend were out by the pool when I arrived home. I went in to take something for the headache and to try to make my pale, tear-stained face presentable. Libby came running in to hug me and say, "I love you, Mommy!" and dart back out to finish a movie with her friend. How I wanted so much more from life for my two blessings.

Richard came home and asked me to talk in the garage which was the only place the girls wouldn't hear us. We had many talks and fights in that garage over the years. I explained that I had a bad headache and didn't really want to argue now. Richard told me that he had been trying to reach me all afternoon. He commented that he could tell I had been crying and asked me to come sit in his lap. He took my hand and began to apologize for his terrible words, actions, and excessive drinking in the past and present. He didn't try to blame me or make excuses. I sensed he was being truly sincere and bearing his soul to me. I wanted to give him another chance, but we had gone through these cycles so many times. Then he told me that he was promising to be the husband and father that the girls and I deserved. He wanted to be loving and kind. He had never made some of these promises before. He told me that he was done with drinking and being with any drinking buddies that would bring temptation to his life. I had been waiting 15 years to hear these words. What had happened? Richard told me that God was talking to him while he rode around in his truck that day. God told him to quit running and set things in order with me. He realized that I was a strong woman who had stood by him all these years, even when he didn't deserve it. We were both sobbing as he told me that he did not want to lose me. I praised God that I had gone to the pastor that day rather than giving up and asking for a divorce. Richard seemed to be taking responsibility for his problem for the first time ever. Could this be what I had been praying for all these years?

I felt that God had removed all the anger, resentment, and hurt from my heart at the meeting with the pastor. Now He seemed to be filling it with faith, hope, and love. The next several months were almost heaven compared to the life we had been living. Richard seemed to be keeping his promises. We were going to church and vacationing together as a family, just the way I had always dreamed. We even shared more intimate time together. I felt like it was a dream from which I never wanted to wake up … my dream come true.

Chapter 8:

THE BIG "C"

Our days became happier and less stressful with quality time for family and even some much-needed time to relax out by the pool, soaking up the beautiful sunshine. I felt more comfortable leaving the girls with Richard now that God had been working in our family. I scheduled our yearly physicals, as well as a trip to Disney World. Right before summer vacation, Richard got a call from his doctor's office saying that his lab work showed high PSA numbers which was indicative of prostate problems. I had only heard of prostate trouble in older men, and Richard was only 40. The doctor wanted him to see a specialist immediately, so I went online and made him an appointment within the next 48 hours. Richard was still hearing

God's voice as he rode around at work during the day. We knew that God would get us through this new trial. Richard did not want to worry the girls until we knew more.

I went with him to the appointment. The specialist was the same age as Richard and also had two young girls. He was concerned with the test results which were so rare in a 40-year-old man. He suggested some other scans but told us he was sure it was cancer. I was speechless and scared, fearing that cancer would take a third person from me. I didn't think I was strong enough to go through this again. Would God really turn things around like this and then allow Richard to die? I closed my eyes and silently prayed while partially hearing the doctor's plans if his suspicions were confirmed. Surgery? Radiation? Long-term effects? Riding home, I felt emotional and numb at the same time. Richard wanted to wait for the test results before we shared this with anyone.

So many thoughts battled in my mind over the next two weeks. I began to see God's hand in all of it and realized sickness was an attack of the enemy who comes to steal, kill, and destroy. Good things come from God, not evil. I repented for being angry with God and began to pray like I had never prayed before. Then we returned to the specialist for Richard's next appointment.

As we sat in front of the specialist for the second time, he confirmed the diagnosis and his plan to set up the radical surgery. The surgery provided a good chance to remove all the cancer, which was a good outlook. I took Richard's hand and prepared for the battle as tears ran down my cheeks. On the way home, Richard told me that he had peace and knew God was in control. I had waited 15 years to hear this coming from his mouth, but I never realized the circumstances we would be in when it came.

We told the girls that Richard was sick but didn't reveal that it was cancer. Soon after we received the diagnosis, he began to lose weight and his dark skin became pale and gray. The surgery was more radical than expected, but the specialist shared at a follow-up appointment that he got all the cancer. However, he would want to set up more scans to be sure within the next few months. I felt like I was living a secret life again, keeping my emotions under control and protecting the girls from the truth. Richard's doctor was holding off on any further treatments until the next PSA, which they would perform within six to eight weeks after surgery. Richard was very drained both mentally and physically for a while but began to improve. After several months thinking we were cancer-free, we made a trip to a local theme park. Richard started back to work part-time in the evenings, and his parents, along with Aunt Dolly, began helping with the girls. Richard began drinking wine rather than beer as it was considered healthier, but the drinking increased.

Two months later his specialist came into the PSA check appointment with unwelcome news. Despite all their efforts, the cancer had spread. He suggested immediate radiation treatments but couldn't guarantee how effective it would be. With a burdened heart, he honestly told Richard to get his affairs in order and spend time with his family. It seemed he felt that the cancer had won. Tears flowed uncontrollably, and I wanted to run out of the office screaming. I felt numb and cold as the hopelessness seemed to overwhelm me. Why, God? Why would you let cancer steal another loved one from me? Would I be left a widow with two young girls? Richard was ready to tell the girls about his prognosis that same day. He would decide on radiation soon. We just held hands and cried together all the way home.

After many tears, Richard thanked me for staying by his side all these years. He knew it wasn't easy, and no one else could have done it. God gave him his Tennessee Angel to love him unconditionally. He wished that he could go back and do things differently and undo all the hurt he had caused. I felt the fear and regret in his heart. I had to be strong for him and the girls again. We had been more a family in the last few months than we had ever been before. I had to hold onto my faith that God had good plans for us. Faith is hoping for things that seem impossible to men but are not impossible for God. I had to trust God.

I picked up the girls from school and sent them to get snacks before we had our family meeting. I was continuously praying as it seemed the room was covered by a thick cloud of darkness and despair. As Richard gently told them about the cancer, they seemed unmoved. Victoria revealed that Richard's parents had been talking about it in front of them with his cousin a while back. They had known for several weeks. I couldn't understand this nightmare, and Richard grew very angry. He called his parents and blew up about the incident. I burst into tears, apologizing to the girls and explained why we hadn't told them. By dinnertime, we had all calmed down and laughed and talked together.

It was hard to stay positive in the days and weeks that followed. Richard decided against the radiation, and he began to decline, rapidly losing weight and drinking more. He seemed to have given up, as though he had stopped fighting. He stopped going to church, and the girls didn't want to go without him. I decided to take them to a Wednesday night youth program at a different church as I really needed to immerse myself in some Bible study with other believers. The first night was so refreshing for me. I felt a new hope rising, and the girls immediately found friends and good youth pastors. When we went home, Richard had a change of heart about the radiation, and I felt like God was working again. He started treatments the next week and went to church with us that Sunday.

The girls seemed to be growing and blossoming. I solicited prayers from everyone I knew including some local churches. The whole community got word of our family's battle with cancer, and love began to pour into us through phone calls, messages, and cards. That kiss from God gave me so much encouragement.

Any time the enemy attacked me with doubt and fear, I would go to the Word of God. I had to trust His truth no matter what my eyes were telling me. Richard began to decline again during the treatments. He was extremely pale, and his bladder was trying to shut down with awful spasms. He told me often of his regrets and his love for me, trying to say goodbye as he felt death coming on him. He decided to make his funeral arrangements, and even though I wasn't ready to give up, I supported him and his decision. Aunt Dolly and Uncle Willis went along with us to the cemetery. I was shaking so intensely that I nearly collapsed. It brought back the memories of burying my mother and brother. I felt as if someone else was controlling

my body as I could only pray silently. When the sales-
man talked Richard into buying two funeral plots for
the both of us, I thought, "Why not? I feel as though
I am dying already." Richard went to bed early that
night, and I watched a movie with the girls and held
and snuggled them. I decided to make the most of all
the time we had left as a family—supporting Richard
and the girls and being strong for them.

Richard and Jezebel had been distant for a while,
but he felt we should meet with her and her family to
let them know what was happening. I called Jezebel
and arranged for her and all her family to meet with
us. I then prepared myself for any drama that might
arise. They knew Richard had been sick but weren't
aware of the severity of it.

We met with them at their home. I held Richard's
hand as he gave them the details. Jezebel, who had
already been drinking, began a very emotional out-
burst, and I moved her outside. She was grabbing me
and shaking me in a frenzy, yelling that she had always
loved Richard. I tried to calm her, but she became angry and screamed in my face, "No, you don't understand, I LOVE HIM! It should have never been YOU!
I don't know why it wasn't ME!"

I felt too mentally exhausted to try to continue
calming this self-centered woman who had clearly
never befriended me or respected my marriage. I

gathered my family in the car as I stewed over her and her involvement in our marriage all these years. Once at home, I went out back alone and repented to God, asking Him to forgive them and the abomination they had caused in our marriage. I also asked forgiveness for myself for being an enabler. Richard came up beside me to ask if I was all right. He apologized for it all. I just rested in his arms and let it all go.

During the break in radiation treatments, Richard was approved to go on a family trip. He had been improving so much. His bladder was working better, his color was returning, and he had been eating without feeling sick. We decided to go to Savannah and Charleston and stay in two bed and breakfasts that the girls helped me choose. Richard had promised to only have a beer with dinner but not drink heavily on the trip. The girls had an adjoining suite so Richard and I could spend some time together alone. It would be the first time we would try to be intimate after all the treatments. There was no pressure, though.

On the way down, Richard picked up a case of beer at the market. He said it was for the entire trip and that I shouldn't worry. I was sure he had already packed some alcohol but decided that I was not going to start an argument at the beginning of our trip. We arrived at the grand, historic home with its solid doors, large windows, and fine antiques. The girls immediately found the two swings in the beautiful garden area. I was glad to see them getting along so well and bonding. Both suites had beautiful high-post antique beds and dressers with a hutch to match. Each room also had a huge fireplace and a fainting couch. Our suite had two antique wingback chairs facing the fireplace. We set up to have our breakfast out on the balcony that the two rooms shared. Richard had two glasses of alcohol at dinner, and I wondered if he was feeling a bit nervous about our time together tonight.

When we returned from the restaurant, we found both beds turned down with mints, and the bed in our suite had been dusted with rose petals and chocolates. There was also champagne on ice on a table by the bed. This made Richard angry, as he said I was pressuring him to have sex with all of this and he went out to get his cooler. I told him that I did not order the special treatment and went downstairs to find out about it while he took a beer out on the balcony. It ended up that the champagne was included in the honeymoon suite which happened to be the one in which we were staying. I had overlooked that detail but thanked the sweet hostess and went back up to our rooms. I took a soaking bath in the huge tub and came out to find Richard in bed. He had spent hours on the deck drinking and now he wanted to pop open the champagne. I sipped a bit to make him happy and told him that my only expectation was to be held and loved. He began to get passionate in his sloppy, nearly drunken way. I was trying to let him take the lead and go at his own pace when suddenly he rolled over and got up with an angry look. He said that I was expecting too much from him. He grabbed another beer and took it out to the balcony. After checking to make sure the girls were still asleep, I went out to check on him. Without looking at me, he called me a hurtful name and told me to go back to bed. I burst into tears and cried myself to sleep.

I awoke to voices several hours later and found Richard sitting and talking with a young man on a balcony adjoining our balcony. Richard introduced me to Steve who was there on his honeymoon. I encouraged Richard to come back to the room as I felt sorry for the bride whose honeymoon had gone so amiss. He did come back inside before breakfast was delivered the next morning and acted as if nothing had happened. I knew that I looked like the one who had been partying all night with my swollen red eyes. I was determined not to ruin the rest of the trip knowing that, in Charleston, we would all be sharing a room together. I quickly packed us up to move forward.

I was feeling very irritated and flew off the handle when Victoria smarted off to me. Richard came to her defense, and then she was upset with me. He stopped to pick up more beer on the way to Charleston and was seeming a bit buzzed as he sang and rolled down the windows. I was concerned that he would draw attention to himself with empty beer cans in the car, but he told me that I needed to relax and let my hair down. The girls carried on with him singing, so I finally joined in too. We arrived at our next B&B in downtown Charleston by Rainbow Row. We were in an old, historic hotel this time with two full-size beds, a table and chairs, and a TV. The hotel had a dining area with a private dance floor and a bar. I wanted to avoid eating dinner there as it wasn't a good family atmosphere, with many old men drinking at the bar. Richard again just criticized me in front of the girls for being a stick-in-the-mud. I tried to hide my tears and be pleasant for dinner. Richard left for the bar when we arrived back at our room. I watched some TV with the girls and fell asleep, waking after midnight to discover Richard had not returned.

I told Victoria that I was leaving to look for him and not to open the door for anyone as we both had keys. I felt sick leaving them alone but knew that I must go look for him. I found him wasted at the bar. He told me to go back to the room, and he would be there shortly. Victoria was wide awake and upset about her daddy when I got back to the room. We both lay awake for a while waiting for his return. I awoke again at 3:30 a.m. Knowing that the bar had closed, I decided to go look for him once more. After searching to no avail, I went back to bed and quietly cried myself to sleep.

Richard came in at 7:30 a.m., reeking of alcohol and looking like a mess. He said, "Well, hello sleepy-heads!" to the girls, and I asked where he had been all night. He said he met a fellow Republican who was having an election party and he lost track of time. I got the girls up for breakfast and left him to sleep. I was battling a headache brought on by stress.

After breakfast, I took the girls to do a little shopping at the local boutiques. Charleston was one of our favorite places to visit, and I usually found really cute clothes for the girls on our trips. We headed back to the hotel after noon and found Richard standing in the lobby looking around. He told us he had rested and showered and was waiting for us, but in my spirit, I knew that he wasn't being honest. We went back out to the marketplace for some lunch and more shopping. Richard and the girls got bored before I was finished, so they took off together. I met up with them an hour later at a bar with a pool table and loud music. Shocked and speechless that he would bring our girls to this place, I told the girls we were leaving. Both of them became upset with me and began to defend their dad. I was beyond furious and spoke harshly to them, which did not help my case. They calmed down, and we did some more shopping. Richard met us in the room for dinner, and then we went out for a carriage ride. He drank heavily the rest of that trip, but I kept quiet to make the time as peaceful as possible for the girls.

Back home, I tried to let Richard have some space and I found serenity in spending time reading the Bible. Then one day he called me from work and told me that he had been visited by the Lord. He knew he needed to change and spend quality time with me and the girls, even if he didn't have much time left. He wanted to take me on a trip to San Francisco where he had spent much time while in the military. The girls could stay with his Aunt Dolly and Uncle Willis, and we could spend some alone time together. I felt like God had answered my prayers and remembered God's promise in Jeremiah 29:11:

"For I know the plans I have for you," declares the Lord, "plans to prosper you and not to harm you, plans to give you hope and a future."

I planned the San Francisco trip along with another trip with his Aunt Dolly and Uncle Willis, who wanted to spend time with us under the circumstances. We had some extra money from selling another business venture when Richard got sick. I wanted him to spend the money on whatever made him happy.

In San Francisco, we stayed in a grand hotel full of antiques and memorabilia of historic and famous people. It would take weeks to view all the floors of history, not to mention the exquisite ballrooms with their large pillars, chandeliers, and tables set up for royalty. We ate our meals in these spectacular ballrooms. Walking through the massive, wooden, double doors was like entering a fairy-tale castle banquet room set with crystal, silver, and fine china, with servants waiting on you hand and foot. Up on the rooftop, which was reserved for hotel guests only, we strolled through garden areas filled with statues and fountains. I had never stayed in such a fancy, grand place.

We had breakfast and dinner at the hotel while lunching at quaint restaurants in the city or out on the wharf. Richard and I spent much time talking and walking and even being intimate together. Richard was still quite weak and tired easily, so he took frequent naps while I read. I was fearful that this would be our last trip together but continued to pray that God would give me more time with this wonderful man that I knew was there all along. On our third night there, I agreed to go down for some dancing with the live band. They played a mix of blues and jazz and even a little Beach Boys. Richard and I slow danced to one of our favorite BB King songs. I felt like the world stopped for a moment and I was in heaven.

Eventually, though, I developed a headache and needed to go lie down. Richard, who had been drinking some, told me he would be up shortly as there were only a few people left in the bar. I awoke at 2 a.m. and went to look for him, but my headache was worsening. I walked all the hallways and checked all the lounges. I looked up on the roof and out into the surrounding streets from the rooftop view. I cried and prayed and started searching all over again, knowing that he was in a frail state. I needed to lie down, but all the sirens and police just increased my fear about our location and all the crime associated with it. I paced until my feet hurt and my head felt like it would blow up. I tried to distract myself by looking at the memorabilia as I walked the halls, but the stress was too much. I finally stopped by the front desk as I had many times that night and told them I would be in the room if they saw or heard anything. I knew I needed to lie down before I blacked out.

I cried myself to sleep, only to be awakened at 7:15 a.m. when Richard came in. His clothes were all wrinkled and he reeked of alcohol. I jumped up with my head still aching and asked what happened. He said he got lost about four blocks away and it took him all night to find his way back. He went into the bathroom to shower and dismissed the other questions I asked him from the doorway. I had to lie back down because of the pain in my head. When I awoke four hours later, the pain had finally receded to a dull ache. I showered and went downstairs for brunch, sitting at a table alone. I tried so hard not to dwell on thoughts of where Richard had been or who he had been with. There hadn't been any single women left in the bar when I went up to the room the night before. We didn't speak much on the plane ride home as he had a bad hangover. I really wanted to cancel our next trip but knew that at least his Aunt Dolly and Uncle Willis would be along, and he wouldn't act up.

Richard and I seemed distant after the San Francisco trip. I found myself trying hard to keep away from him as much as possible to keep the peace at home. The workdays were busy, then suddenly our next travel date was upon us. We had vacationed with Aunt Dolly and Uncle Willis before and were all staying in the same room with two double beds. This gave me a peace knowing that Uncle Willis could keep track of Richard this time. We usually went to Mexico together, but this trip was to Las Vegas. I had never been to Vegas and knew that it was a casino town. I had gambled a few times and had considered myself lucky in winning, but I didn't truly understand the addictive qualities of gambling or the consequences of immersing oneself in the darkness that usually ruled in these cities.

When I played the casino games in Vegas, I felt a rush of excitement, hoping for a win. I tried to relax and have fun and forget about my problems. I was using the games as an escape like some people do when they drink or get high. Richard left with Uncle Willis to hang out at the bars while Aunt Dolly and I played blackjack and the slots. Time went by so fast with the men checking in with us every now and then. Before we knew it, we had played through dinner! We took a break to eat and do some sightseeing among all the tinsel and lights. I decided to pace myself as we had two nights to go, and I had dedicated only a certain amount of money to use for the casino games. It was well after midnight when we went back to the hotel to lie down. I awoke in the morning to find Richard missing.

I took my shower and went downstairs to look for him. Richard came up behind me in the lobby and grabbed my waist. He asked if I had spent all my money yet, and I asked if he had spent all his on alcohol. He told me that the alcohol was free. I should have guessed that drunk people would spend more money. His Uncle Willis and Aunt Dolly showed up, and we had breakfast. Aunt Dolly and I went to an older hotel and played slots through lunch. The men came back hungry, so we left together. I had been having a carefree time knowing that Uncle Willis was staying with

Richard. That night we played a little blackjack, and Richard suggested that we go walking on the strip. We encountered many ladies of the night, both young and old, some brave enough to hand their cards to our husbands even though we were together. I was truly shocked by it all.

Richard led us through the streets to a black building with no lighting around it. It felt very eerie and evil to me. It was filled with very loud music and strobe lights that were bothering me. Aunt Dolly, Uncle Willis, and I waited outside while Richard went in. He came out 30 minutes later and reluctantly left with us. Aunt Dolly and Uncle Willis went back to the room at our hotel, but Richard and I stayed up for a while. I wanted to play a few more slots, and Richard went to the bar. I lost track of time playing my favorite wheel game. Uncle Willis came looking for Richard, but he couldn't find him. I had last seen him drinking and laughing at the bar with some guy. I went back to the room around 1 a.m. expecting to find all three of them there already, but Uncle Willis had returned without Richard.

I really didn't expect Richard to vanish with his aunt and uncle there with us. They were beginning to worry and wanted to get the police involved, so I felt I had to tell them about the other trips. I shared how Richard would disappear from the bar on our vacations and come back in the early morning hours very drunk and disheveled with a strange excuse. I could see Uncle Willis hang his head in shame, probably assuming Richard was cheating. I told them that he never smelled like women's perfume or had any lipstick evidence on him when he returned, but I never found out where he had been. Aunt Dolly grew angrier as I told them the details with tears streaming down my cheeks. They had seen more of his erratic behavior on this trip than they had seen before. Nevertheless, he was like a son to them, and the worrying increased as the hours rolled by. Uncle Willis went out to look for him several times to no avail. I finally fell asleep right before he returned around 7 a.m. Aunt Dolly met him at the door with angry words as she had been through this herself. She assaulted him with questions about his whereabouts and his selfish attitude for about twenty minutes with no backing down. Uncle Willis then took him out "for a walk." I apologized to Aunt Dolly who quickly let me know that I had nothing to apologize for. Richard was the one who should take the blame.

I showered and thought through everything that had happened. I felt a sense of fear and overwhelming hurt. Aunt Dolly told me that "you knew if your man was cheating," but I didn't feel I had all the evidence to convict him. I had to ask her to talk about something else as I felt the lack of sleep and stress might bring on a seizure. I knew she wanted to help me and pull me out of this bad situation, but she had never really been able to help herself out after all these years. It would be a long day awaiting our flight home tomorrow.

Chapter 9:

A NEW LIFE WITHOUT YOU IN IT

Upon returning home, I was close to making a decision to seek a divorce. It pained me to think of the girls growing up with this separation, but now it seemed better than the alternative. Richard's PSA levels had gone down, and it would take a year to see if he was in remission. The girls were already starting to distance themselves from me as Richard was constantly manipulating things to make me look mean, serious, and condemning. I had kept so many things from the girls to protect them that they had a cloudy perception of their father. I had to be the girls' disciplinarian, acting as both father and mother most of their lives. Richard was always the fun parent who acted more like a favorite uncle to spoil the girls. It was easy for him to make me look harsh and controlling.

I suggested counseling as a last hope, but Richard refused, stating that it didn't help me last time. He later relented, and we decided to see one of the girls' therapists. We also had another trip to Mexico scheduled for spring break that I truly feared taking. Our family of four was scheduled to go with Aunt Dolly and Uncle Willis. We had never taken the girls out of the country, and I was scared after hearing stories of kidnappings and worse. Richard assured me that all would be fine as we had been there so many times in the past. It had always seemed a safe place, plus we would also have his Uncle Willis and Aunt Dolly as an extra set of eyes.

Spring break came and we arrived in Mexico where the girls were able to see all the beautiful places they had only seen in photos. Richard began drinking immediately. His aunt asked him to slow it down, but he just said he wasn't "hurting anyone" and just liked "to have a good time." Then as if I weren't right there, he said, "Don't be like Angel; you should be having fun!" I tried to have a good time with the girls, seeing the sites as Richard drank the trip away. We were able to swim with the dolphins, visit a zoo, and shop at the local markets. One night I had an allergic reaction to seafood at dinner and my throat began to swell. It was only a brief scare, but I couldn't bear the thought of leaving my girls in a situation like this! After cleaning the condo one day, I found Richard and the girls out by the pool. The girls were then 13 and 11, and Richard had bought them their own "virgin" drinks. I was completely livid about this inconspicuous introduction to drinking and the generational curse. All these occurrences continued to point me in the direction of separation.

The final straw that broke the camel's back came two nights before we left. The girls were in the hot tub out back and Richard got in with them ... completely drunk. He turned up the music loud enough to bother the neighbors and began to talk about vulgar topics in front of the girls. It bothered Aunt Dolly so much that she left to go inside. I turned down the music and reminded Richard that he was not with his buddies but with his daughters. He turned the music back up and continued to speak with profane language and vulgarity. I told the girls to go to bed, at which point he turned on me with his usual criticism and some choice words.

After I went inside, Uncle Willis went out to talk to him as he continued to call me every name in the book. I went back out to turn off the music, and he called me names and told me that he and the girls couldn't stand me and hated me. I went back in the bedroom and didn't realize he had followed me. I soon found my-self hanging up against the wall with his hand on my throat and my feet dangling in the air. His eyes were full of blackness and rage as he threatened me. I was fighting for breath and to get loose, realizing that no one else was there to help me. He finally released me and said, "You disgust me!" I ran out of the room and into the living room crying. The girls were sleeping in there, and I wasn't sure if they had heard anything. I knocked on Aunt Dolly's door. As soon as she saw my neck, she sent Uncle Willis to tell Richard he had gone too far. I tried to cry as silently as possible but felt a migraine or seizure coming on. Uncle Willis told me that I could go on to bed, and Richard would stay outside.

I finally got to sleep and was awakened the next morning as Richard came in the sliding door. My neck was still red and my eyes were puffy. He asked me to come out on the balcony and talk. I could tell that he slept in the lounger and had already had his coffee. He said that he loved me and didn't know why I made him so mad like that. I began to cry knowing that this wasn't love. I was sure that he was incapable of lov-ing anyone, even himself. I let him know that I was going to look into divorce when we returned home, as he clearly had no remorse over what he had done last night. I was done! Libby hugged me at breakfast, but Victoria just gave me a cold stare. I just wanted to get home. We bought the girls some cups with strobe lights at the airport which caused me to have a seizure. Richard had to nearly carry me to the plane. I slept the entire flight.

Upon returning home, we made an appointment with the therapist. As soon as we sat down in her office, Richard's eyes became black with darkness like the night he grabbed my throat. With vulgar words, he informed me that he had already filed for divorce and he would be keeping the girls. He gave an evil laugh and told me that I was getting what I had always wanted and that I was the one to blame. The therapist just sat there. Richard followed me out to my car taunting me. I called Liz who said she would set up an appointment for me with a lawyer. With no family members left to support me, I was so thankful for Liz and a few close girlfriends to lean on. I went by the school to find that Richard had already picked up the girls and taken them to his parents' house. He and his parents had been talking more right before and after the last trip.

I wanted to get home to get the gun before Richard could use it on me in a drunken rage. I then went to meet the lawyer, as Liz had made an immediate appointment for me. I felt like I was in shock and fear that this was really happening. I kept seeing those black eyes and hearing the maniacal laugh. I didn't know what he was capable of doing in that state. It seemed that evil had finally taken him over. I revealed all our secrets and dirty laundry to the lawyer who agreed to take my case. I didn't tell her about the recent physical incident, but I knew she could sense my fear. I told her that I wanted to spare the girls as much hurt as possible. I hoped Richard and I could both parent the girls from different homes. She drew up some papers that I signed, and then I went home. Richard and the girls were out by the pool. I went in to gather a few things to move to Libby's room for work in the morning. Confusing thoughts were going through my mind as the only life I knew was being a wife and a mom, and all this seemed to be changing rapidly. I wasn't sure if the man I loved still existed at all, or if this evil creature was actually the man I married.

I went out to the pool and asked to talk to Richard. Victoria gave me the cold shoulder as she huffed away. I hoped that we could sit the girls down together and tell them gently that we both loved them, and they didn't need to choose between us as we would make things for them as easy as possible for them. I knew we could be kind toward each other to keep the common goal of loving and supporting our daughters. Before I could speak, Richard informed me that he had already talked to the girls, and they had both decided to live with him. He wanted to make that clear up front. I couldn't understand why he would do all this. Then I remembered Richard being deeply affected by the divorce of a friend who had to take a second job to pay child support to his ex-wife who got the house and the kids in the divorce settlement. The wife did not let him see the kids either. Richard talked about all of this for a very long time.

Richard's tone suddenly changed from calm to evil as he began unleashing profanity, calling me vulgar names and taunting me, telling me how I was out of the house and left all alone. He said he couldn't stand me, and he was keeping the house and the girls. "I'm the one in charge here, and I say what happens!" he screamed at me. Shocked at his words, I yelled back at him that he was a liar and that our girls would not be used in this divorce by either of us. As I rushed inside, he continued to call me some of the worst names a man could call a woman as I rushed inside. I passed Victoria in the garage fearing she had been eavesdropping. It made me feel sick that she heard all the vulgarity. I was becoming so angry even though my heart was breaking. My head was swirling as I tried to comprehend what was happening. I shut myself in the bathroom looking at the dirty commode bowl and thinking that Richard's mouth and heart were even dirtier. I then did something very disrespectful that

I quickly regretted. I took his toothbrush and ran it around the commode rim and put it back as I heard him coming in the house. I had never done anything like that to anyone before and quietly asked God to forgive me.

As I passed him, Richard was announcing to someone on the phone that he was going to bed. He then made some sickly sweet comments to the girls about wishing he could stay up with them, but he had to get up early for work. He would spend time with them tomorrow. I decided to go sit outside for a bit to collect my thoughts. I invited the girls to come, but they didn't respond. I knew how Richard had gotten to Victoria and prayed that God would protect Libby from the manipulation. God was my only hope. Here I was again putting all my trust in Him. I had spent years of my life sacrificing my own interests and desires for the man I loved and my two girls, but now I didn't feel like praying for this marriage any longer. I felt my skin was thickening as I determined not to be defined by Richard's harsh words. I slept in Libby's room that night, dodging all the thoughts running through my mind.

Richard came home the next day and called the girls away to talk privately. I assumed he had been served with his divorce papers. I had asked for full custody of the girls because of his alcohol problem.

My lawyer also included some restrictions preventing any alcohol or drinking around the children by him or others. This would help keep our home safe for the time being. He continued to drink in spite of this, and I would find many empty alcohol bottles hidden in various places. Richard even kept a cooler in his locked truck to keep the alcohol hidden. My lawyer had me take pictures of this for evidence before the trial.

The papers I was served from Richard's lawyer accused me of lying, cheating, and child abuse. I didn't know at the time, but Richard had fabricated a story that I had cheated on him and broken his heart. This drew the sympathy of many people for him. Day by day the environment grew worse. The girls began pulling farther away from me, although I could tell from the look in Libby's eyes that she was being forced by fear tactics.

I ended up moving down to the guest room in the basement after about a week. This room had a key lock, and I had the only key; yet several times I found Richard standing over my bed in the early morning hours with eyes full of evil. Richard stayed in our bedroom where he left the photos of our family and removed the photographs of the two of us from the dresser. He wanted to make it seem to the girls as though he was having a hard time with our separation.

They did not hear the terrible comments he made to me in whispers and when they were not around. He would call me to dinner and then act hurt if I didn't want to eat, playing off the rejected spouse so well.

Richard was manipulating the entire situation to make me look like the instigator of the divorce and breakup of the family. I knew that God was not riding in the truck with him anymore. He had truly turned himself over to the enemy. At one point, I heard Richard talking to the therapist on the phone and realized that they were building a case against me using some private conversation I had with her. This was to convince the judge that the girls should stay with him. I prepared to turn her in for this as she was breaking her privacy oath, but it never got that far. Richard's family were all backing him as if they had been a close-knit family all along. Richard also suddenly became interested in being a school parent to make a good impression, although he was turning the girls against their best friends.

I really missed spending time with the girls, but Richard had convinced them to distance themselves from me. Libby would love on me briefly if the other two weren't around but would act as if I didn't exist at other times. Victoria was so full of anger and hate toward me that she would even try to fight or hit me. Richard became very irrational and would frequently go into rages, acting out and yelling for me to go back to my dungeon where I belonged. I chose to walk away and fight back in prayer for the girls' sake. When he hurled slanderous lies at me, I only responded by saying, "God knows." My heart felt sick about all the lies our daughters were being told as he worked to turn them against me. I prayed that God would be my advocate and remind them of my character and my love for them. I felt helpless to do anything on my own.

One day, Richard called me out to the pool area to tell me that since the girls had decided to stay with him in their home, they wanted me to leave. I was in shock at this proposal. Libby would not look at me, but Victoria glared as she told me she was in on this decision. I left crying, with my head swimming as I went into the dark basement. Feelings of betrayal cut into my soul like a knife. I felt so alone I couldn't breathe. My heart was pounding out of my chest, and my mind felt like a runaway train. All the tormenting thoughts were too much to handle. The pain of Richard's betrayal was unbearable. Even in all my anger, I still loved him. This loss was like death. The cancer didn't kill my husband; nevertheless, he was dead. Dead were all my dreams of a healed relationship and growing old together. Dead was my commitment and my marriage. I was grieving with no comfort or hope. Where are you, God? What is your plan in all of this?

The following night, I went upstairs to find Richard and the girls watching a vampire show made for mature audiences. I realized that Richard was trying to take away all the authority I had over the girls' lives. This was not acceptable, so I made my voice heard. I then changed the channel, and Richard stood up to grab and twist my wrist. He declared that he had told the girls they did not have to listen to me anymore. He said that I was done around here and could not come in and change anything. He said, "Get back down in your hole, and stay there!" Shocked, I told him to let me go, or I would call 911. I noticed the strong smell of alcohol as I pulled myself free. I then took the phone outside and called 911 through the barrage of yelling and screaming coming from the house. The police pulled in with Richard's brother right behind them. In the meantime, Richard had popped a fresh bag of popcorn and was eating it quickly to hide the smell of alcohol. I told the police my story and they instructed me to go downstairs as they spoke to Richard. Victoria told the police that I started the argument and then tried to get Richard to hit me. I went to my room in the basement and the police left without doing anything further. Richard, his brother, and the girls appeared at my door to gloat, with Richard saying that my tricks didn't work, and they were glad the police saw the truth. When the others left, Richard stayed behind and spoke his message with vulgar words in a hushed tone: "Your days are numbered, and I will see to it that you pay for that incident. Sleep really good, honey, as everyone knows you are crazy now!" He laughed in that evil way as he left me to cry myself to sleep. I felt alone and as though this would be the reaction I would get should I need the police again.

Chapter 10:

FIGHTING FOR THE TRUTH DURING ALIENATION

I began to see clearly that the alienation was starting. It seemed that the girls were being "brainwashed." This was a military tactic Richard had described to me long ago. It seemed that hate and anger were beginning to fill their minds to replace any good memories they had of our past together. My daughters refused to go to work with me anymore, and Richard demanded that they be taken to their grandparents' house instead. He would even take them there on my weekends with them. Richard continued to remind me that they did not want to be with me, and that he was protecting them from me. I still did not know what lies he was feeding them. I continued to trust in God even though I could not see His hand at work. I found comfort in the words of Habakkuk 3:17-18:

"Though the fig tree may not blossom, Nor fruit be on the vines; Though the labor of the olive may fail, And the fields yield no food; Though the flock may be cut off from the fold, And there be no herd in the stalls—Yet I will rejoice in the Lord, I will joy in the God of my salvation."

As the court date continued to be postponed, I tried to spend some time with friends who could encourage me. Looking back, I am overwhelmed at the support God sent me through friendship. My grandparents and good friends were my lifeline to hope. I had my special prayer warrior, Lila, along with Liz, Tay, Marie, Ann, Thelma, Lou, Bea, and Harriet. All of them were there to give me strength through the journey.

I learned at this time that Richard had been planning to divorce me—and had even been working with his attorney—ever since we returned from the Las Vegas trip. I decided that I needed to leave the house when Richard's behavior became even more evil. He began to verbally threaten me and break into my locked bedroom, leaving the door open to let me know he had been in there. He wrongfully filed an order of protection against me and even listed himself as the only parent when signing our daughters up for school. One weekend, out of fear, I went to my friend Lou's place with just a few items and the clothes on my back. My friend Tay took me back to the house to get some clothes for work. She continually tried to get me to take more of my things feeling like I wouldn't be coming back. I assured her that we could come back later. Libby had been continually texting me asking where I was. Sadly, I knew that Richard was the one trying to find out my whereabouts. Tay took me back to Lou's house. I wasn't sure where I would go now as I had used all my money for the lawyer. Just then, the phone rang. It was Liz offering me a place to stay for the next few weeks. What a blessing!

A hearing was scheduled with a judge who threw out the order of protection against me and gave me rights to pick up my daughters at a public place for our weekends together. He also agreed that they should still be going to the counseling appointments I had already paid for. I began journaling while at Liz's place and started attending Al-Anon meetings which helped me to see my situation more clearly. I also started a Divorce Care class at a local church.

Richard still kept me from the girls and he didn't allow me to pick up my belongings from our "marital residence," as they now called it. He had his friends and family follow me to track my whereabouts. All I did was go to work and meetings and, although I felt unsafe, I continued to go. My friend Marie found me a furnished place to stay. It was in a safer location than Liz's home and had everything I needed. I took different routes back from work every night to keep the stalkers confused.

Richard began swaying and manipulating the girls' new counselor just like the last one. When he was drunk, he used to tell me how weak and easily manipulated women were. Now I watched it playing out before me. I prayed for everyone involved, including Richard, as the Lord reminded me of Luke 6:28:

> " ... *bless those who curse you, and pray for those who spitefully use you."*

My God was again my greatest comfort and counsel during all this.

We finally got a court date set, and my attorney was demanding to know my address as I needed proof that I had an apartment with a bedroom for my daughters. I went to bed the night before court so stressed and tired of the system. I was awakened by the Lord in the early morning. He led me to read Matthew 25:33:

> *"And He will set the sheep on His right hand, but the goats on the left.*

I wasn't sure what this meant, so I awaited more understanding.

I met my attorney the next morning and saw Richard arriving with his family and the girls. My heart broke to know that our daughters would be present. My attorney and I were seated on the left side of the room, when I remembered the verse God spoke to me. Was I sitting in the goat's spot? Then I saw in my mind's eye the judge's view. I was seated on the right from that viewpoint. I was so glad to know that I was one of the sheep of the Good Shepherd, and I would follow His voice and His leading. I began to weep knowing that He would take care of me.

The court proceeding was long and full of false accusations and lies. All the stress resulted in my having a seizure, after which Liz and Thelma took me home. As I rested, I looked in brokenness at my wedding rings. I couldn't help but remember the day Richard placed them on my finger, and we said, "I do." I knew that I still loved him as I tried to get the courage to remove the rings. It was time, so I removed them. I cried myself to sleep, wanting to hold my daughters in my arms again.

The next day I looked at a nearby apartment and signed a lease to move in within the week. I borrowed the deposit and first month's rent from Liz until my paycheck was released. My friend Ann gave me a cot and air mattress, and I used my credit card to get some sheets and a blanket. I picked up some toiletries at the dollar store and stopped wearing makeup as it was too expensive for me. Marie donated an old TV and stand to which I added an old indoor antenna. Thelma and her husband brought me a used washer and dryer and extra towels. All this love from my friends restored my hope as I could see God at work providing for me.

I was spending much time reading my Bible and keeping a record of dates to remind me of how many times God had resolved problems and answered prayers. I journaled my thoughts and events daily to purge them from my mind. Even though I was being encouraged, I felt darkness trying to overwhelm me, especially at night. The stress and pressure combined with the enemy's attacks on my mind in the empty apartment made me feel helpless. Thoughts of Richard's plans and schemes floated through my mind since I knew he was using his family and their financial support as puppets in his life of lies. It was hard to continually choose forgiveness each time these thoughts arose. The evil forces wanted me to believe God had forsaken me. My mind would become foggy and confused, and I didn't know how to pray. Nevertheless, I held to the truth that God would never leave me or forsake me. I knew He was fighting for me, and I would see it in His timing. Even though I couldn't understand why He was delaying justice, I remembered the words from Isaiah 43:1:

"Fear not, for I have redeemed you; I have called you by your name; You are Mine."

It was clear that retaining the house and all its belongings was Richard's main goal at the expense of our daughters' lives. The date arrived when I was finally allowed to get my belongings from the house. Richard was not allowed to be there but, on my way, I saw him hovering nearby in his truck at a red light. I could see his black, evil eyes as he threw his head back in a silent maniacal laugh. I asked God to take all the love out of my heart that I had for this man as he was no longer the man I had married. It happened suddenly and left me feeling empty but peaceful. I didn't hate him, but now I only felt the compassion of a Christian for a lost unbeliever.

As I pulled up, I saw Richard's mother and his Aunt Carol standing by the open garage door. Inside the garage were the things I had asked for. My friend Tay came as a witness along with the police for protection. I felt overwhelmed while walking back into the basement to retrieve my clothing, personal items, and a few pieces of furniture. I felt defiled knowing everything had been searched and picked over. The worst part was knowing that I had to leave my precious daughters there for now. As I left with such finality, I prayed that God would break all the generational curses, and that both my daughters would learn to receive the love of their heavenly Father.

The day finally came for Victoria and Libby to spend time with me at the apartment. I felt a bittersweet excitement not knowing what to expect. In order to have them stay with me, I had to have a place for them to sleep. I used my credit card to buy a mattress for them. Not seeing the girls was the hardest part of this separation. My lawyer had advised me to quit asking for custody as both girls had told their counselor that they wanted to stay with their dad. I was told Victoria had even said she would kill me in the night if she had to stay with me. I still knew in my heart that they were God's blessings to me, and I would not give up on them. At the apartment, Libby kept her distance along with Victoria, but her eyes revealed how much she needed me and loved me. Victoria acted up the entire time, arguing and smarting off. Later, Richard's attorney picked apart our visit and said that only Libby wanted to return. I was only to be given occasional lunch visits now with Victoria.

A little over a year after the initiation of the divorce proceedings, I found myself unable to pay all my bills, as well as the child support I'd been ordered by the court to pay to Richard since he had temporary custody of them. The country was in a recession in 2008 and my income was greatly decreased. I couldn't even find a second job as no one was hiring. I began to ask God for direction and guidance when Thelma offered to let me live in her second home on their farm for less rent than I paid for my apartment. What a blessing!

It didn't take long for mysterious visitors to begin showing up. They would just pull up at night or sometimes during the day in vehicles with tinted windows. They sat in the main driveway watching me in my new residence. Thelma began locking the gate to their property to help keep me safer. Not long after, Richard's lawyer sent a letter demanding my new address "so Libby could visit." When I picked up Libby, she revealed that she already knew where I lived and had been to see it. Nevertheless, we had some wonderful visits together. Libby was such a different girl without anyone manipulating her words and actions. Although the counselor asked Richard not to interrupt our visits, he and Victoria constantly texted Libby on her new cell phone. Although it seemed like this would never end, I knew by faith that God would end it, and He would seek vengeance on my behalf. No matter how much Richard could manipulate the system, God was not blind to the truth. He sees all, just as I said to Richard from the beginning. I held to Proverbs 3:5-6:

"Trust in the Lord with all your heart, and lean not on your own understanding; In all your ways acknowledge Him, and He shall direct your paths."

As the court battles carried on into the next year, Victoria still did not meet with me or recognize me as her mom. When she turned 16, Richard bought her a car with his tax return money and put her to work. She confided in a mutual adult friend that she had to work to help her dad out as he could not make it on his own. The friend later told me what Victoria had said, and that she seemed angry and unhappy. Hearing this had me in tears. I felt that she had become the new enabler for his lavish lifestyle. As Richard's lawyer continued to delay the court case, the assigned judge died, and we had to wait for another to be appointed. This required more funds and seemed like I was starting all over. Marie helped me get a part-time job which provided extra money for bills and child support. What a blessing!

I texted the girls morning and night to remind them of my love but never received any responses from them. I looked forward to our Christmas celebration together, which would be two weeks after Thanksgiving. It was like heaven as the girls and I spent several hours baking cookies together and decorating the tree. I also gave them their gifts. I never imagined that it would be our last Christmas together. God sent my friend Tay with a special invitation for me to join her family for Christmas Eve and Christmas day. That was such an unexpected blessing.

Richard soon stopped my visits with Libby by saying that one of my friends was speaking against him in her hearing while she visited. Both the counselor and my attorney agreed it was for the best, but I knew that was not God's will. The only weapon I had to fight with was prayer. I felt so mentally and physically fatigued that I decided to let God fight for me. I looked forward to the coming of spring and a release from this dark winter.

As everything began to bloom, I got a call from an old friend, Rose, who invited me to come visit her for a few days while her family was out of town. Rose had known Richard and me in our early days of marriage and partying, and she had had to pull away from us at one point to keep her family safe from all our problems. Now she offered to pay for my food and gas if I could come see her, so I jumped in the car and headed her way. God used a special song, "I'm Letting Go" by Francesca Batistelli, to release me from some of the burden as I drove that day. The weekend with Rose was just what I needed. I'm so thankful for good Christian friends who listen when God speaks.

After the short reprieve, I went back to more paperwork for the case. All the financial strain was bleeding me dry. I didn't even have money left for groceries. Thankfully, Thelma and her husband invited me up for dinner often. Day by day, I went to work and came home awaiting the day God would set things right. I continued to stand on Jeremiah 29:11 along with Romans 8:28:

"And we know that all things work together for good to those who love God, to those who are the called according to His purpose."

Richard could no longer afford the house and decided to purchase another home in his name. This left our old house empty and unkept while the attorneys fought back and forth over whether he would agree to sell it to me and at what price. After many deceitful acts, Richard gave me permission to pay him half of the house value and I alone would own our previous home. I wasn't sure how I would feel living there again after all that had happened. The whole process dragged on a long time, so I continued to live at Thelma's house while waiting on the closing.

Thelma's daughter Anna and her boyfriend Andy adopted me as their companion and spent weekends with me watching movies and eating pizza. I cherished the time they spent with me as I missed my daughters so much. Andy continually encouraged me to meet his dad, who he said was a "good man." I couldn't see why I would need another man when I couldn't even get free from the last one.

One Sunday at church, I gave my last dollar in the offering plate. I felt so low as I listened to a sermon from 1 Samuel 30 where David and his army came back from battle to find that their families had been carried away captive and their city burned. This was a shock to David and his men. They cried out to God, not knowing whether their families were dead or alive. I felt defeated and shocked like David. My family had been taken from me by the enemy, and I didn't know if I would ever be reunited with them. The pastor went on to explain that in the midst of their terrible situation, "David strengthened himself in the Lord" (1 Samuel 30:6). I decided to truly let go and do what David did—trust in the Lord!

The next morning, my body shut down and I fell to the floor. The medical report read "stress and total shutdown." I awoke in the ICU with Thelma's head on my arm as she cried and prayed for God to have mercy on me. I was aware she was there, but I was in a peaceful place talking to God. I was telling him that I would rather be with Him than remain here on the earth in this situation. It was too much to bear. Everything I knew had been stolen from me, every person I had loved. I could no longer find my identity as a wife and mom. I felt barren and empty without purpose. I knew my enemy, the devil, was responsible for all this. He had taken my destiny and won. I wanted to go home to heaven where there are no more tears and sorrow. I wanted to stay in this peace. Suddenly, I began to see myself on the hospital bed again with Thelma. God told me, "I am not finished with you yet. You will return to do my good works on the earth. I will never leave you, even in the darkest hours."

My eyes fluttered as I returned to my body and Thelma began to cry, saying, "Thank God, you scared us to death. Please, don't do that to me again." Her husband had found me unconscious when I didn't show up for work. He thought I might be dead. The ambulance picked me up, and my father was called in. I ended up in ICU for three days before being released.

I regained strength in the days that followed. Tay and Thelma arranged for a trip to Mexico for my 40th birthday. Tay would accompany me, and we would not talk of any stressful issues. We would be free to enjoy ourselves. Toward the end of the trip, I felt that I wanted to write a note to Richard since we weren't allowed to talk in person. I used the hotel stationery and prayed before I wrote:

> "My heart has been broken by the loss of loved ones. It has been torn apart and forever scarred down deep. All those years I thought something was wrong with me, that I needed to change, but it was you all along. The life we were living

was my dream and your nightmare. I thought you were a normal man who loved his wife and held his marriage as precious as I did, but it is now clear to me that you were just along for the ride. I could hate you for taking 20 years of my life, but cannot because of the two special gifts I have received from the time of our marriage. All of the lies and accusations will never stop me from loving our daughters. I will love them and be there for them as long as I am on this earth. You may never know the pain your manipulation has caused me, but I suspect you will one day because in life you reap what you sow. You may have damaged my personal and professional life, but God holds my heart and soul. I do pray that someday you will see that God is in control, and that He is what is truly missing in your life. I hope you will turn to Him."

I folded the note and quietly put it in my suitcase without waking Tay. I wasn't sure if Richard would ever read this note, but I needed to write it to move forward. I was not a puppet on a string for the enemy to control and play with any longer. I was finding my new identity in God and His plan for my life. I knew healing would begin, and that my wounds and the pain would one day be gone.

I soon had another invitation to visit my friend Wendy in Georgia. Each time I really needed to get away, God sent an invitation through friends. I spent much time resting and watching TV. It was relaxing but a bit stiffening as I wasn't used to the inactivity. One day, before we left the house to do some shopping, I received a mystery call from my home area code. A strange yet familiar man's voice began to speak. What he told me caused me to sit down on the stairs and freeze. "Your husband is gay." He told me that the gay community was unhappy with the way Richard was using the girls and thought it was time that I knew the truth. Anger, hurt, and disbelief filled me as I began to process this information. My mind recalled all those times that Richard had disappeared over the years, and how confused I felt because I didn't know where he was. I felt like such a fool as it all started making sense. It was hard enough thinking he was with another woman, and now to find out it was another man! I felt a scarlet letter "S" for shame attaching itself to my chest. I went back and forth blaming Richard, myself, and God who could have intervened. I began wondering if he had been with Teddy who had died with a suspicion of AIDS. I would need to be tested for all the STDs.

Wendy found me bawling and babbling in the stairwell. She wanted to know what was wrong, but I felt I needed some time to myself before I could talk about this with anyone. The next morning, I tried to make small talk with Wendy, but I broke down under the pressure and spilled it all out. Wendy was shocked as I released all my worries and fears of this exposure and how it would affect me and my girls. I never knew that gay people could lead a double life like that. Maybe he had pretended to be straight and had married me to make his family happy. Whatever the reason, it was a cruel and devastating deception!

After returning home, I met face to face with Liz to get some advice. I didn't want to talk over the phone because I was worried about it being bugged. Liz revealed to me that she could see the signs all along. How could I have been so blind! I knew that it was love that blinded me and an intense dedication to my vows and my family. Liz agreed to keep my secret for now. I also had a visit with my grandparents and confided the secret to my grandmother. She thought I shouldn't tell anyone. I prayed all the way back home for my girls, who would soon learn the truth. I asked that they eventually would overcome any bitterness and anger with God's peace and joy.

Chapter 11:

SOMETHING FROM NOTHING

Even though I knew that I had been deceived, I could still feel the scarlet letter of shame burning on my chest. I sat down in my attorney's office and gave her the details of the phone conversation. To my surprise, she laughed as she realized how the puzzle pieces fit together. She had been over the case so many times and couldn't make sense of it. Although I believed the girls would want to be with me after hearing about this, my attorney felt that they had been fed too many lies about me that left them hating me. She also didn't want to ask for more visits for Libby, as she felt that the request would be denied. I left her office realizing that I could not put my trust in the corrupt legal system that was full of injustice and criminal rights. I knew with God's help my honesty and integrity would be recognized eventually.

Lying in bed one night, I began asking God to bless me with a male friend. I was so thankful for my faithful crew that had been encouraging me, but they were all couples, and I felt like a third wheel rolling along beside them. It also seemed they were starting to feel weary of my upkeep. It had now been two years of these never-ending divorce proceedings. I had so many male friends through the years who gave good insight and wisdom to me. I valued those friendships and felt it was time to ask God to choose one for me. I wanted my shattered heart to be able to love and trust again.

Work was still slow, and my finances were at a critical low point. I was also feeling unstable in my emotions. I cried often, remembering the past, and I sometimes wanted to shut people out to hinder further chances of rejection and abandonment. God would remind me through His word that He would never abandon me. Isaiah 49:15-16 says:

"Can a woman forget her nursing child, and not have compassion on the son of her womb? Surely they may forget, yet I will not forget you. See, I have inscribed you on the palms of My hands; your walls are continually before Me."

I realized about this time that I wanted to find out my true identity. For years I had been relying on Richard and others to tell me who I was. I had just passively fallen into the role that was spoken over me. Now I wanted to know what plans God had for me. I found myself reading the Bible and absorbing so much. I reread my past journals and chose to forgive each offense and be free of any bitterness. I even asked God to forgive those who had hurt me. When the enemy tried to remind me of those events, I would say out loud, "I rebuke you, devil, and in God's name you must flee!"

I began to seek the joy of the Lord. I began to see colors in a new way and found that I really liked turquoise and brown. I also began interceding for my girls in a new way, not out of fear, but out of authority. God began to answer these prayers and confirm them in ways that were just for me. It was like getting a hug from my Father. This love could not be matched by a human being; it was incomparable.

The day came when I would return to walk through the house that I had not returned to since Richard had moved out. Lila prayed with me the night before as I was dreading the memories and what I would find when I arrived. She reminded me of Romans 8:31:

"What then shall we say to these things? If God is for us, who can be against us?"

Tay would be meeting me there with a garage door opener she was picking up. I took some old clothes to change into after work which included a comfy T-shirt, some spandex workout pants, and my worn-out tennis shoes. I knew many items at the property required maintenance to get them up and running again. I was preparing myself for whatever I would find. Getting out of the car, I felt a heavy weight on my shoulders and a huge lump in my throat. Dread covered me like a dark, weighty cloak.

I broke down as I entered the unkempt mess inside. I had tried to keep both the inside and outside of our home in perfect condition while I lived there; now it looked more like the dark secret of the life I tried to hide. Everything was in disrepair, and most of my belongings and paperwork were discarded in the basement garage. Again, the state of this home mirrored the way I felt, rejected and abandoned. I felt the stress turning into a migraine. Tay hurried me through the rest of the house and took me back to her house to lie down. I looked at my swollen eyes in the car mirror along with my hair all disheveled and tight in a crazy, new curly perm. It was a good thing I wasn't seeing anyone anytime soon.

I took some migraine pills and slept at Tay's until the phone jolted me awake. It was Anna asking where I was. I had forgotten about the dinner date I had planned with her and Andy, and I was 30 minutes late! I tried to get out of it, but she wasn't taking no for an answer. My eyes were a bit better, but I still looked like a hot mess. Thankfully those two young people had already seen me at my worst. I tried to put on a big grin as I walked into the family-style restaurant. They waved me down, and I found them sitting at a table full of people I didn't know. Anna told me that this same group met every Tuesday night to visit and eat together. They called themselves the "Club of No Life." I ordered an unsweetened tea because I couldn't eat after the migraine. After about an hour, it was just me, Anna, Andy, and a man named Lee who were left.

When Anna and Andy left, Lee and I continued to talk for a while. I had not realized he was Andy's dad until Lee called him "son" as they were leaving. It suddenly hit me that this was a blind date planned by the kids! I looked at this handsome man, and then looked down at myself in my old clothes with puffy eyes and a wreck of a wild, curly perm. I let out a loud chuckle and stated that this was probably the worst I had ever looked. He actually told me that he liked the way I looked, and that he was dressed by his son to come to this date. We both just laughed together thinking about all the plans of the kids to get us here. He was so easy to talk to that I felt I had known him my whole life. We talked for hours and I didn't want the night to end, but the restaurant was closing, and I started a new job in the morning. Our vehicles were the last two in the parking lot. I looked up at the starry sky with bright stars that reminded me of my loved ones smiling at me from heaven. What an amazing night in contrast to the dreadful day I had experienced. Lee commented on my beautiful smile which made me blush and sent butterflies fluttering in my stomach. It was minutes before midnight when he asked if he could call me, and we exchanged numbers. He hugged me, and I returned the embrace feeling so safe and protected. It was hard to let go and return to the real world. Then he kissed my forehead and said, "Good night." I felt all tingly as I floated to my car.

My phone rang as I was driving home, and it was Lee. We talked all the way home and another 45 minutes after that. I lay in bed trying to sleep as my thoughts were all over the place. What am I thinking? I am still married! Yes, the divorce proceedings had lasted for two years now. I wondered if I was rebounding, but then remembered the request I made to God for a male friend. Was He answering so soon? I felt like I needed to guard my heart, but I also usually had good judgment about a person's character. Lee truly seemed truthful and genuine. I fell asleep trying not to fall in love too quickly and thinking this fairy-tale meeting was too good to be true.

The next morning, I received a "Good morning" text from Lee and floated into work thinking of last night. I felt like I had bounced back to my joyful self. Throughout my life, I would bounce back to joy after trauma, but it had not happened during this divorce. It seemed I had built a stone mountain around my heart because of all the rejection, and I wasn't sure that even God could break through it. Even if the relationship with Lee went no further, I was glad to be free of heaviness. I was seeing everything with a new mind-set. Marie asked about my smile, so I told her all about my evening. The encounter with Lee gave me a hope that life could go on after this divorce and that God still had plans and human relationships for me in the future.

Over the next few days, Lee and I texted back and forth some, but it was less than I expected. Maybe this was only a friendship for now. Trying to hold back my hopes for more, I decided to just keep going and see what God had planned. I was invited by Anna and Andy to a giant car show the following weekend. I hadn't seen Libby in three weeks now, and I needed some human companionship whether Lee accompanied us or not. Anna and Andy were a blessing from God. I found myself doing things with them that I would have never done otherwise, and I really enjoyed myself each time. They picked me up alone, and we started out to the show. They asked me about Lee and I played it down, focusing more on how they embarrassed me by the surprise when I showed up dressed the way I was. I was puzzled when they pulled in at a small house with a work truck parked in the driveway. I quickly realized we were picking up Lee! My heart leapt with excitement!

I knew in that moment that God had heard and answered my cry. He had not only sent a friend who had a pure heart, but one who was handsome too. It seemed we could talk about anything and never grow tired of each other. I felt a new journey was starting in my life, and my heart and soul were being restored. God's Word and promises never fail!

We walked from one end of that giant car show to the other as I left a trail of glitter behind us from my sparkly shirt. Lee and I talked non-stop as if we had known each other our entire lives. I found out his family was from my hometown. He told me stories of his family and his hunting days. We laughed so much, and I could see his lovingkindness and contentment. I even felt comfortable around him when my squirrely, goofy side came out. Lee would just smile, and my heart would pitter-patter at the thought of a man I could be myself around. When we parted in the early morning hours, he came and hugged me, and I felt the butterflies dancing inside me again. Then he leaned over and kissed my cheek. I knew I was blushing and floating again.

My friends and even my attorney could tell a difference in my demeanor and attitude. Even though I had a court date coming up, I wasn't nervous and anxious like normal. I really felt God sent Lee to me at that time as a support for the continuation of the divorce trials. Then he seemed to pull away.

I discovered Lee was afraid we had jumped the gun while I was still legally married. He was concerned that it might be God's plan for Richard and me to reunite because he was dragging things out. Lee had tried to work things out with his wife after she cheated. It had been a bit of a roller coaster, but his divorce was quick yet still very painful. He shared some of his deepest pains with me including the love and heartache he had for his children who were the true victims of divorce. We realized the commonalities in our "unequally yoked" marriages. We had each acted out the part of both parents in our separate marriages, and Lee was also alienated from his children during the divorce proceedings. We both wanted to do things God's way the next time around. I told Lee that I really hoped we could remain friends as friendship is what I really needed right now.

The week passed, and we continued to talk on the phone. Libby responded to my weekend request, and

I was overjoyed! I knew the court date was next week, and it seemed that they were following protocol; but, either way, I couldn't wait to wrap my arms around her and love on her. I used the credit card to pick up some groceries for her. Lee texted me a few times during the weekend, but I had him listed under a female name. Libby always asked to see my phone while visiting so I often deleted anything that might seem like evidence that could be used against me. I especially did not want Lee to be involved in this divorce. My lawyer was weary of the case just like I was. Richard and his lawyer continuously played games delaying court and scheming to get more money. It seemed that they had some kind of internal spy that would get wind of our arguments before court cases. Because I wasn't sure who the mole was, I was suspicious of everyone and kept my trust with my small circle of friends.

Libby and I got up early the next morning to eat at her favorite buffet before going to the library. She absolutely loved the biscuits and gravy there, and it was reasonably priced at just under $5 per person. We didn't take the time to dress up as we weren't planning to see anyone. I was completely shocked to see Lee sitting with a friend at the restaurant! We didn't speak to each other, but I realized that this was the second time I looked like I had just rolled out of bed. Libby could see the expression of joy on my face both times I saw

Lee and asked, "What's up?" I covered by telling her how much I enjoyed being with her, which was also true. She had already noticed a change in my emotions and attitude. I wanted so much to tell her about Lee, but I knew that would be a mistake at that time.

I got a few texts from Lee as Libby was choosing books at the library. That restaurant was one of his favorites. He didn't seem to notice how unkempt I had looked. Then Libby and I had a great walk around the park seeing the wildlife. I texted with Lee a bit more that night while Libby was reading and spent one more day with Libby uninterrupted.

On Tuesday, I went to the "Club of No Life" meeting to meet up with Lee, but he wasn't there. He texted that he was on the way about two hours later, so I waited around with his friend Lola. She was having some of the guys over for cookout in a few days and asked if I might want to join them. She left Lee and I alone after he arrived. He ordered an unsweetened tea for me without my asking. He was so thoughtful. Each time we were together, I knew that we would fit together so nicely. We stayed until closing again and spent the time deep in conversation. When he left, he gave me a sweet but quick hug in the parking lot as we could see a storm coming our way. During that embrace, my heart melted as I realized how respectful, stable, generous, and amazing this man was. I was getting more confirmation that God had chosen this man for me.

Lee and I texted daily and met several more times at the restaurant on Tuesday nights. I also went to Lola's for the cookout. I knew Lee was a true gift from God, but I still fought guilt that the divorce was not finalized. One night, I rode with him on a work call up into the mountains. It was dark on the way back down, so he took my hand to comfort me. He told me that his job working on power equipment took him into dangerous places, but he knew God would protect him. Lee always made me feel calm and peaceful. He walked me to the door and told me that he would like to take me on a real date, maybe dinner and a movie. Then he reached over and put his hands around my waist and hugged me. I was blushing and floating as he pulled out of my driveway.

The next weekend was my time with Libby, but she didn't come. Instead, my nephew Dane came to stay with me for the weekend. I helped raise Dane after my sister divorced his dad when he was still a baby. Lee invited us both to a barbecue and overnight stay at the lake, along with Anna and Andy. We all had to sleep in a loft with one bed, a couch, and several air mattresses. Lee and I had our first picture made together that weekend. Dane seemed comfortable with Lee, and the two had a great time talking on the trip back.

It was so easy to talk to Lee, and he didn't seem to mind my squirrely way of jumping from one topic to the other. His joy and peace seemed to be real and independent of his circumstances. I began to feel increased shame, though, that I had never mentioned to Lee that I found out Richard was gay. I knew that Lee had felt the same hurt of having an unfaithful spouse, but I wasn't sure how this new revelation would affect him. I knew that we both had a strong moral compass which was very important to me, but I was so afraid Lee would leave after hearing about Richard, and I wanted to spend as much time with him as possible. Eventually, I would need to share everything with Lee, but I prayed for the right timing.

Our first date arrived on a Saturday night. I was so nervous knowing that we were moving forward in our relationship. I really felt that Lee was my best friend. I really didn't know what this handsome, stable man saw in me, but I was so grateful that God brought him into my life. I blushed when he told me how beautiful I was, and the butterflies began swirling in my stomach. We went to Lee's hometown so I wouldn't see anyone I knew. We laughed and chatted all through dinner, and then we headed to the movies. I was too full from dinner to thoroughly enjoy the movie popcorn that I loved so much, so I decided to eat less next time. I felt warm and tingly inside when Lee reached for my hand during the movie. We also held hands back to the truck where he opened the door for me.

We talked all the way home, and I found out that we frequented some of the same places with our kids when they were younger. We passed a "gentleman's club," and I made a comment about Richard saying that the place was nasty. I was interested to hear Lee's response. He said, "Is he gay?" I was silent for what seemed like a long time. I said, "I have been told he is by another gay man." Without missing a beat, he responded, "Only a gay man would say that place is nasty." I was breathing easier knowing that the cat was out of the bag, but then I began to cry uncontrollably. He apologized for offending me, and I told him how embarrassing it was to be rejected in marriage by a man who turned gay. He laughed and replied, "Angel, he is crazy if he could ever pick a man over you. No real, worthwhile man would ever make that mistake." He reached over to take my hand and kiss it. That was when I knew I was in love with him.

When we returned to the house, Lee came around and opened my door and helped me out. He put his arms around me and told me that I was amazing and beautiful and that there was nothing for me to be ashamed about concerning Richard's bad choices. He leaned in and gave me a gentle, sweet kiss as the sparks began flying, and the butterflies went wild, setting off a tingling flurry all over my body. I wanted that moment to last forever.

Lee came over for dinner the night before my court date. He passionately kissed me and asked if I wanted him to go with me to court. I could see the concern in his face as I told him no. I froze with my head against his chest, with a new concern for him. I didn't want him pulled into the madness of this divorce. At the same time, I felt so free going into this court session as I knew that I was loved by this man. I had never felt so passionately loved in this way, and I knew I would remember this moment as long as I lived. I knew that God had answered my prayers in a way that I could never have imagined.

I met my attorney alone the next morning, and quickly learned that our daughters had been removed from school yet again to testify against me. The trial had to start all over again with this new judge who was old and had come out of retirement to handle some cases after the first judge died. I was called to the stand first and kept there for over three hours as Richard's attorney tore me apart, along with my reputation. My attorney just sat there amidst this circus, running up billable hours. Although the girls had already been signed over to Richard, they were demanding three times the state-recommended child support, so the trial went on and on. I looked out at Richard's relatives knowing that they would one day feel deceived when they found out Richard was gay and all these accusations were lies. My heart especially cried out for our girls, and I prayed again for their protection and provision. Richard's lawyer had him on the stand for 30 minutes, portraying him as a saint while my attorney did nothing. I left feeling the weight of the corrupt justice system yet again.

I went straight to see Lee as I felt a migraine coming on. I fell into his arms sobbing, and he held me for a while. Then he picked me up and set me down in a new place. He said he was lifting me out of the "box" Richard and his attorney had placed me in and declared that I would not get back in it again. I agreed as he helped me lie down on the couch with the migraine. I awoke hours later to Lee's fearful look. He had come close to calling 911 after the seizure but remembered that I told him that I needed to rest and sleep afterwards. He talked to Thelma who coached him through what to expect, and he made me some food from his freezer for when I awoke. I asked him for a half peanut butter sandwich instead, as I needed the protein. I ended up staying there overnight with Lee sleeping on top of the covers to separate us as he watched over me. Before he left for work in the morning, he smiled and gently kissed me, then he told me to rest, make myself at home, and please never do that to him again. I got up to try to prepare for work in two hours, but instead decided to call in and lie back down. Walking into the bathroom, I noticed that Lee had laid out fresh soap and towels for me, along with a new toothbrush and toothpaste. For a man, he kept the bathroom very neat. By the time he called to check on me, I was feeling much better. He told me where I could find some peanut butter and crackers and asked if he could bring me dinner tonight. I was so overwhelmed by the blessing of this amazing man. I turned on the music channel on TV as I ate. The song "God Gave Me You" by Blake Shelton was playing, and I sat there and thanked God for all He had done for me. He gave me Lee at the best possible time, and I knew He had great things in store for us.

Chapter 12:

HAPPINESS AND ABUNDANCE

I would soon be moving back into the house vacated by Richard and the girls. The holidays were coming up, and this year would be Richard's time to spend with Victoria and Libby. Lee had invited me to spend the holidays with him and his family, so I knew I wouldn't be lonely. I also planned to spend some time with my grandparents as my grandfather's condition was worsening. I really wanted them to meet Lee and give their approval. They also told me that they wanted to encounter the reason for "all your smiles."

The weekend before our visit to my grandparents' house, Lee and I discussed moving our relationship forward. After months of friendship, we were growing closer than I ever imagined. We were truly best friends. His respect for me and my godly morals made the transition to dating easy and flawless. I knew that he would not pressure me to have sex before marriage as we had discussed this previously. I had two requirements for continuing forward: Lee meeting my grandparents and the two of us attending church together. Lee had been saved as a child and had been to church off and on since, but he felt he always had a spiritual compass in life and could talk to God anywhere. I explained that we really needed to meet with God regularly just like we need food to survive. He pondered this for a while and smiled. Then he agreed to attend church with me when he wasn't working. I knew that I must be bold about my convictions and relationship with God up front. Remembering the battles with this in my previous marriage, I planned to stand strong in my conviction that God came first. If God brought us together, Lee would be in agreement with me.

The visit to my grandparents' house went wonderfully. They both welcomed Lee with open arms and made him feel at home. He mentioned on the way back how much alike my grandmother and I were. She reminded him of his own Memaw. Because all his grandparents were dead, Lee felt privileged to spend time with mine. He told me he would be by my side from now on. We laughed and talked all the way home.

The next few months flew by. Lee began going to church with me regularly, and we spent much time together through the holidays. I gave him a shirt, and he gave me a gift card saying that he wasn't good at choosing gifts. I stuffed the presents and stockings for the girls into the large mailbox at their house. After the holiday whirlwind, it was time for me to move into our old home.

It was a stressful time with moving, the mess left at the house, and wondering how God would provide for all my needs. Nevertheless, I knew He had always been faithful and would continue to be. I also was blessed to have help from my dear friends. Lee and Lila brought others to help on moving day. My grandparents loaned me the money to get the electric and water turned on until I got my next paycheck. Thelma's husband helped change the locks. Lee agreed to keep the pool in order and help with groceries as my business was still in recession. Little by little, everything was falling into place.

I texted Libby who was turning 15 this year to see if she wanted to come stay with me for her weekend visit and, to my surprise, she said, "Yes." Lee really wanted to meet her, so we set up a cookout for Saturday with several of my new friends, including Lola, Tim, Andy, and Anna. Lee would bring the food. I was nervous and excited for Libby and Lee to meet, praying that

Libby would like him. The evening turned out great! Libby was her bubbly self at the party, and everyone loved her.

Lee asked Libby if he could take the two of us to a movie the next night, and she agreed. They chatted together throughout the drive. On the way home, she urged me to sit in between them, and they talked and laughed over me about the movie. I could not have asked for a better time. I knew how much Libby loved this kind of fatherly attention, something she never received from her dad. I thanked God for all He was doing.

Before he left, Lee asked Libby for her permission to take me out. She laughed and said that it was about time. She thought we were made for each other. Later, she told me he was a really great guy, and she was not planning to report this to Richard. Then she kissed me goodnight, and I told her I loved her. With a grateful heart, I thanked God for all of us and the way He was weaving the old and new together in a beautiful tapestry.

I began cooking for Lee in the evenings, and he and Andy began to help me out at the house. We all worked together so well, which was foreign to me. One night on the porch swing gazing up at the stars, Lee told me that no other woman had ever made him feel this way. I looked into his eyes and told him that I felt the same and never knew it could be this way. We were so happy to share our love with each other.

My Sunday school class had been through the thick and thin of the divorce with me. Although I was the youngest in the class with most of them over 65, they had been a great support and wealth of encouragement, especially Wendy. These special people had prayed with me for Richard through the cancer and then throughout the court trials. They had been watching me grow stronger over the last months and were now embracing Lee. Wendy poked me and whispered, "He's handsome." I blushed and nodded. They were my "church family."

I still struggled with the fact that my girls were no longer in church. I was thankful that I had a chance to give them a firm foundation while they were little. I hoped that it would bring them back one day. They learned about the love of Jesus and the blood He shed on their behalf so they could be forgiven of their sins and spend eternity with Him. I also felt I had given them a strong moral foundation. I was sometimes tempted to think that I had failed, but I knew I did the best I could. I knew I couldn't dwell in the past and needed to keep moving forward.

Lee and I continued to grow closer and spend more time together. I sometimes stayed over at his house if I wasn't feeling well or if it got too late to drive safely. Knowing my convictions, he never tried to have sex with me. I never even had to worry about him pressuring me. He was completely considerate of my choice to wait until marriage. One night while I was there, he kissed me goodnight and told me he loved me. I told him, "I love you, too." We kissed again, smiling and laughing, and we both knew it was true. We were in love.

Lee continued to take Libby and me out on the weekends. She must have kept our secret for a while because we hadn't had any backlash from Richard or his attorney. We got the pool up and running and painted Libby's bedroom sunshine yellow. Lee and Andy installed a fence and a gate to give me a sense of security. My friend Annette helped me with some decorating. Everything was turning out so well.

Then, one weekend after two amazing days together, Libby began to seem distant as she texted back and forth with Victoria. She told me that Victoria was coming to get her before her time with me was up. Victoria parked at the neighbor's house, and both girls left without saying goodbye. I found out later she told the neighbors that she had come to rescue Libby because I wouldn't allow her to leave. I was left feeling heartbroken and confused. That was the last time Libby came for her weekend visits or any visit … not for my holidays, or summer vacation, or Mother's

Day. Somehow Richard had been able to alienate me again.

On a positive note, the school added me back to the girls' paperwork and would call to let me know when special parent events took place. I went to every one possible. Thankfully, the principal and staff knew of my integrity from all the years I had been the only parent involved. I was so thankful that someone could see through Richard's charade. I praised God for this. I spent much time praying for the girls and all aspects of their lives. Not being able to speak to them, hug them, or even communicate was tearing me up. My friends and Lee were so faithful to lift me up when these circumstances brought me down. Friendship was the best gift God could have given me at this time.

Lee stood by me in court from that point on. The newest judge ended up being the best one. If only we could have started with her. The trial would soon be over after more than three years of lying and deceit. Things began to move more quickly, but the attacks from Richard increased, especially after he saw me and Lee together at a gas station. I was able to handle everything better now with Lee at my side.

Lee took me many places I had never been before, living up to his words: "Stick with me, baby, and I'll take you places." I felt God's love filling me up through Lee even though I missed my daughters; their absence was a great loss in my life. But I knew that the road to my destiny had veered down a different path, and I was excited to see where it led. By putting God first in our relationship, we were growing closer to Him and each other.

I was constantly amazed by how God was blessing me. I knew the truth from Philippians 4:13 which says, "I can do all things through Christ who strengthens me." I was always getting compliments from Lee now, and it was hard for me to accept them. I had some fears that I would build up this dream only for it to come crashing down. I knew that time would tell, and I continued to pray for wisdom. God's peace was sustaining me and giving me grace to hope. I knew He had good plans for me, and I was determined to continue in that mustard-seed faith.

It felt like all my dreams were coming true. Lee and I had been together for well over a year by now. He was showing me God's unconditional love in human form. We spent our weeknights and weekends together. I also spent much time with his large family who had given me a warm welcome.

I finally went to my last court date, and the divorce battle was over. It was the last time I had to hear words of death and destruction pour out of the mouth of Richard's attorney. Everyone thought I should be ecstatic to be done with the divorce but, truthfully, I was only numb. I had officially lost custody of my two daughters. I had been granted only weekend visits and would be allowed to participate in health and educational decisions. So much had been stripped from me during this long four-year battle. It seemed for those last few hours in court, much of the battle flooded back to my memory. I had tried so hard to shelter the girls and give them a good life. Now I had to trust that God would take over for me and not allow them to carry the burden I had carried. God's light exposes the darkness eventually, and one day my girls would know the truth. My tears began to flow uncontrollably. Although I was being faulted in part and could see areas where I could have made better decisions, I would never apologize for following God and trusting that He could heal my marriage. As the gavel dropped, I felt an emptiness inside like a great void that reminded me of the loss of my first baby. It seemed that it would remain forever. Even so, I left the courtroom knowing that God was restoring me and creating in me the identity He had always meant for me.

Victoria met with me to get her graduation and birthday gifts. I found out she had moved out of her dad's house and was living with her boyfriend's family. She was mostly house-sitting for them as they were gone a great deal of the time. Libby was left alone with her dad and all his drinking friends for a short time before she moved in with Richard's Aunt Carol. Both girls retained their good grades and were college-bound. I thanked the Lord for answered prayers.

One fall evening, Lee called and came by after work. I was ready for bed in my T-shirt and shorts watching TV. He used his emergency key and hollered out a "Hello, honey!" as he came in. The next thing I knew, he was bent down on one knee smiling from ear to ear and holding a box in his hands. I had to remind myself to breathe as he took my hand and said, "Angel, will you marry me?"

Sobbing and laughing at the same time, I said, "Oh my gosh! I can't believe this!" I leaned over to hug and kiss him and tell him I loved him.

He looked puzzled and said, "Well, will you marry me?"

I laughed and said, "Yes … yes, of course, I will marry you!"

He stood up and said, "Good! My knee is killing me." He swept me up in a bear hug and told me that I had made him the happiest man on earth. He put the most beautiful ring on my finger, a brilliant, deep red ruby, the color of love, surrounded by diamonds. What a breath of fresh air to have him in my life after all these years.

We decided to have a small, intimate wedding with family. This still entailed about 60 people because his family was so large. I went dress shopping with his mom because I wanted my very own dress this time around. I found one at a secondhand store with the tags still on it for only $100, which was exactly what I had saved. (Lee's mom helped me out with the extra three cents.) It fit me perfectly. My friends gave us a wedding shower, and my church friends were over-joyed as they followed our wedding events each week. If anyone had told me this would be happening a year ago, I would not have believed it. This plan of God was more than I could have ever imagined.

Chapter 13:

GETTING RID OF THE DEMONS

As the wedding day drew near, we continued to prepare. We spent some time in counseling with the minister who would marry us, until he felt that we were ready to begin our new life together. He was the family friend who was responsible for leading Lee to the Lord as a child. So many times I wanted to pinch myself to see if this was really happening. Just six months ago, I wouldn't have guessed I would be so in love and making this commitment with a handsome, godly man like Lee. I found myself surrounded by his protection, love, kindness, understanding, and compassion day after day. We couldn't wait to officially become husband and wife. My only regret was that my daughters had not responded to their invitations.

The wedding was beautiful, simple, and intimate. Lila and Annette did an amazing job of decorating for both the ceremony and the reception. Lola prepared the delicious barbeque sandwiches and sides. My dad walked me down the aisle in my new wedding dress to meet Lee and join hearts with him. One special part of our ceremony was the braiding of three cords—symbolizing the joining together of me, Lee, and the Lord—because we had decided to put God first in our marriage. We also released two doves to represent our love for God and for each other, as well as the freedom we were both experiencing through our faith and love. It was a day I will cherish forever.

After helping clean up, we set off to the airport for our honeymoon cruise. Neither of us had ever been on a cruise and were excited and nervous at the same time. We had several hours to laugh and talk on the drive. Lee made me feel so special on our honeymoon. I had never felt so loved and respected. I was nervous about our intimacy, but Lee was so gentle and eager to please. I never knew it could be this way. Our bond wasn't just romantic, but full of mutual respect, devotion, and unfailing love. We also completely enjoyed the beauty of the sights and sounds as we were pampered together. What a wonderful new life with God's blessing.

Once we were home and back to work, Lee and I began to work on house projects together and continue in our family time. We had decided to rent out Lee's house and move into my home together. This was a hard decision, but we realized that my house needed much work before we could put it on the market. Together with Lee, I was making new, good memories in the house that had only held sadness for so long. However, there was still something about living there that gave Lee reservations about staying too long. We spent much time with Lee's family in our first few months together as husband and wife, especially cooking out. I felt so blessed to be welcomed into their closeness.

One day, as we were out driving, we saw a for sale sign in front of a house that got Lee's attention. Apparently, he had dreamed of us owning this home while we were dating, but it wasn't up for sale then. He asked if we could buy it, and I laughed and said, "Can you sign your name?" The house needed much work. It came with some acreage and a detached garage. It was our first large, remodeling project together. We found ourselves in many heated discussions which gave us a bit of testing. Nevertheless, we always made up and learned more about our strengths and weaknesses.

After our first stage of remodeling was finished, we decided to put my house on the market.

We priced the house at a good market value and gave it some great curb appeal. It truly looked the best it ever had, inside and out. Unfortunately, it seemed to be sitting stagnant. I decided to stop stressing and let God handle the selling side of things. We had our church friends praying, and soon we had an interested family. They would need to rent for six months before purchasing, but Lee and I felt good about the deal after meeting with them.

The following week, I had a special women's retreat at my friend Wendy's. I was ready for a stress-free getaway even though I would miss Lee. The retreat was wonderful with much-needed rest and quiet time with the Lord. A few days into it, I got an early morning call as I was headed downstairs for breakfast. I was walking down the same stairwell where I got the call about Richard being gay. The call was from my friend and spiritual mother, Ruth. When she spoke, her tone was serious. She told me she had just had a vision from the Lord about my house. I sat down on the stairs to listen intently, just like I did with the other phone call years ago. Ruth had been awakened by God at 4 a.m. and given a vision that my house had been cursed by Richard before he left. The curse was put on the house and all its belongings, as well as on everyone who entered it. I felt faint like I was in a fog. My body felt odd and my legs were shaky. A curse? Chills ran all over my body as I remembered how Lee felt uneasy about the house. I had also suspected that Richard was using some sort of witchcraft against me during the divorce. Other strange events came to mind like how I had come across a penny and a dime in one corner of each room while I was cleaning it to put it on the market. We'd had problems with a number of items breaking down one by one for a while, and many buyers and agents viewing the home felt something was "off."

Ruth was given instructions as to how we should confront this situation. God instructed her to go to our home with some strong intercessors to pray, praise, and give glory to God in every room. We agreed upon Saturday for the prayer time, and I would ask another couple I knew to accompany us. I was a little confused and fearful as I called Lee. I then spent some time in prayer and repentance for any part I could have played in this, and I also asked forgiveness for those who had participated in this curse. I asked God to cleanse their hearts. I then asked God for peace in our new home and the old one.

After returning home from the retreat, Lee and I asked our good friends Calvin and Leigh to come pray with us. While talking with Leigh at our favorite lunch spot the next day, I got a call from the man who had bought all the pond fish from my house a few weeks earlier. The two hundred fish were from several generations of fish, many of which had been at the house for over 10 years. The fish were all healthy and had just finished their dormant winter season. They were all expected to live up to 20 years longer, but the family buying the home did not want the upkeep of the pond. As I talked with the man, he began to tell me that the fish had been mysteriously dying at each and every location where they had been distributed. No one could figure out what was happening, and no treatment was helping. He called to ask if I thought they could have been poisoned.

On the drive home after lunch, I was in tears thinking that this might also be a result of the curse. I called Lee and we prayed together over this situation. Richard might have done the deed, but I knew that ultimately the devil was behind this darkness. He uses weak people for his plans. First Peter 5:8 says, "Be sober, be vigilant; because your adversary the devil walks about like a roaring lion, seeking whom he may devour." We began to bind up the enemy and speak life and blessing over the house and anyone who entered there. The new family was set to move in within hours of the intercessors coming.

I was determined not to let this curse victimize me. Lee and I prayed again together Saturday morning before meeting with Ruth at the old house. We were expecting that God revealed this darkness to eradicate it. We turned the battle over to Him. We asked God to lead, guide, and protect us as we followed His orders. We asked Him to break the curse and cleanse the home.

As we prepared to leave, Calvin called to say that he and Leigh would be praying from home as he didn't get much sleep and had a bad headache. Lee and I went on to the meeting expecting God to lead us to victory. The house looked dark and empty without any hint of warmth or welcoming. I gave Ruth a big hug as we went into the heart of my old home. Ruth's friend, Sharee, had accompanied her. We held hands as Ruth and Sharee began speaking out to God and then banishing the darkness. They called for the angels of heaven to come fight for us. We started centrally in the living room and continued until every room was covered with prayer. Lee and I silently agreed with our prayer warrior friends, at times feeling the hair standing up on the back of our necks and finally the darkness leaving the residence. It was all very draining. Sharee was so exhausted that she collapsed to the floor after the battle was over. She said that the darkness against us was so strong, but our God was stronger and had won the battle. The darkness would not be back in this home or our lives again. Ruth and

Sharee anointed our home with oil in the name of Jesus and prayed blessings over it and all who would live there. Then they prayed over us.

After our friends left, Lee and I stood in the house holding each other and praising God for what He had just done. We could feel a difference in the house … it was peace. Just then, we heard the family entering from below with laughter and excitement. I wiped my eyes and turned the keys over to them, knowing they would live here in blessing and joy. I looked back at the house as we were leaving, remembering the years gone by. Such a mixture of dreams and heartache, joy and pain, love found and lost. I knew this house had been built on the sand instead of the solid rock of Jesus like we read about in Matthew 7:24-26:

"Therefore, whoever hears these sayings of Mine, and does them, I will liken him to a wise man who built his house on the rock: and the rain descended, the floods came, and the winds blew and beat on that house; and it did not fall, for it was founded on the rock. But everyone who hears these sayings of Mine, and does not do them, will be like a foolish man who built his house on the sand: and the rain descended, the floods came, and the winds blew and beat on that house; and it fell. And great was its fall."

The false world we created in that house and its many secrets made for a great fall. Though I was leaving all shame and guilt behind that day, I would not leave it in the house for the new family. It was time to close that chapter of my life, free from the curse. Our new life was being built on the solid Rock. Lee and I had decided to follow God's path and will for us, and we knew that He would be walking in front of us. I could move forward in the new path to a wonderful life of respect and true love, knowing that one day my daughters would follow me.

Chapter 14:

REFLECTIONS

Lee and I were living a life full of happiness together. It was so amazing to give love and receive it back. For so many years I had given 100 percent of my love and only received a few crumbs in return. I guess some could call it a weakness to love with your whole heart, but now I was receiving the benefits of it.

For the first year of marriage to Lee, I dealt with some old triggers that seemed to be keeping me in bondage. At times I felt like I had made a mistake pulling Lee into this time of working through it all, but God was leading me to freedom. As I spent time with God, He was breaking the power of these thoughts over me. He was teaching me how to resist the enemy. I remembered my mother's words as I was growing up: "Get behind me, Satan. There's nothing that the Lord and I can't handle today!" I felt those words were eerie at times when I would hear her speaking from another room and wondered if Satan himself was standing in our home. Now I was using them myself and growing in my spiritual life.

As Lee and I grew together and served our church and community, people could see our joy and happiness. We bought more properties together and worked on them side by side. We also spent time watching movies, going out with friends, and traveling. We continued to pray that our blended family would have more communication and stronger relationships … especially my daughters. Our children were our most prized possessions, and we knew that God would bring them all back to us one day.

Richard moved out of town which quieted the gossips for a while. His openly gay life had provided many awkward conversations and criticism. He even brought his boyfriend to Victoria's high school graduation. All that emotion and shame of his "coming out" weighed so heavily on me and affected me deep down in my soul. My reputation had been soiled and dragged through the mud, especially when I had been accused of cheating. After Richard left town, I felt like I no longer had to wear the scarlet letter for his sins. Gossip calmed down and better news took the place of our scandal. I met a coworker of Richard's a few years later at the airport when Lee and I were heading out on our five-year wedding anniversary trip. He shared how all the guys were very disappointed in the way Richard handled our marriage and divorce with all the lies and deception. He said that they all supported me and knew the truth. It helped me to see that God was redeeming my reputation.

I always wanted to remember that what others say or do does not determine who you are. It is what God says about you that determines that. Our choices can sometimes delay God's plan, but He is faithful to set our feet back on the path when we repent and return to Him. I prayed that my children would understand that, too.

About this same time, I was learning to wait on the Lord. I had always led the life of a busy bee, wanting things to be done yesterday. God was giving me new perspective with trusting Him and His timing and guidance. He was helping me to sit still and listen to Him. I was learning that I wasn't made to "fix" everything myself, but to turn my burdens and cares over to Him. These revelations might seem insignificant to others, but they were life-changing for me. The Scripture verse Psalm 54:4, "Behold, God is mine helper: the Lord is with them that uphold my soul," always reminded me that God was there to help me in every situation.

Although my life journey had been hard, my God never left me. He fought many battles for me. He also used parts of my story to encourage many others during hard times. Even as I remembered it in the retelling, God was freeing my soul. We overcome by the blood of the Lamb and the word of our testimony according to Revelation 12:11. As I shared the testimony of my life, unseen wounds were exposed and healed by the Great Healer.

It was a joy to minister to others with my new husband walking alongside me. I felt like I had already been given a great reward for serving and trusting God all those years. I remembered the words my brother Al spoke so many times: "Life is good." It was exciting to move forward and see what God had in store.

Chapter 15:

FORGIVENESS

Both of the girls had moved on to college and independent life. As my marriage to Lee continued, many of the triggers—the words, sights, and even smells that left me feeling sad—were fading and gone. I still dealt some with the effects of mental abuse from the previous years. As I lived in a loving marriage, I became aware of the great amount of mental abuse I had suffered before. I began to surrender pride and expectations to God, who I realized wanted the best for me. Everything I could need, desire, or imagine was being provided by Him.

While driving down the road one day, I got an overwhelming feeling that I needed to go to Richard and ask him to forgive me. I quickly opposed this

223

thought. I hadn't seen Richard since our last day in court, seven years ago. He sent me a voicemail right after that, playing the song I had requested for my funeral. I felt I had forgiven Richard and didn't feel that I needed to see him in person. Just in case, I began to speak out loud all the hurts for which I had forgiven Richard and even the places I had forgiven myself. I did not want to carry a burden for that again.

After coming out of an appointment, I again heard the voice of the Holy Spirt urging me to go to Richard. I always rested better after dealing with forgiveness face to face. The Holy Spirit had prompted me to do this many times in the past. Although I wanted to obey God, I had fears of Richard starting drama again. After three months of gentle reminders, I asked Lee to pray with me about it. He would stand beside me through whatever God asked me to do. I also asked some church friends to pray. The longer I waited, the more weight I felt.

One day, driving down the road again, I felt the Lord tell me to call Richard and set up a meeting. I had heard the same thing a week before but didn't respond. I remembered how God had told me to meet with Richard during the divorce, but each time some new accusations would come forth. It seemed impossible to meet with him then without attorneys. Now the path was clear, but fear was so strong.

I comically began to make a deal with God. I would call Richard, but if no one answered, I would hang up. I recalled how Richard seldom answered his phone, even when we were married. I hoped my act of obedience would allow me to obey and move on without actually having to connect with my former husband. As I waited at a red light, I searched for his contact number that I had kept as "contact unknown" after the divorce since I felt I no longer knew him. Unfortunately, the number was not in my phone. Just as I thought I was off the hook, a 10-digit phone number came to mind that I knew was his. This time, I pulled over and called it.

When I heard his voice on the phone, I froze. Then I realized it was the voicemail. I took a deep breath and left a professional message: "Hey Richard, it's Angel. Could you give me a call? Thanks." I felt like I had left an impersonal message for a client. I went home in hopes that he would not return my call. However, as I got settled at my desk, the phone rang, and it was him.

I answered with a sound "Hello?" He immediately replied, "Angel, you called and asked me to call you. Is everything okay?" I responded, "Yeah, I just wanted to see if we can meet and talk." The rest of the call was congenial, and we decided to meet at a coffee shop in between our homes on Sunday at 3 p.m.

For the next several days, I felt anxious about the meeting. Since the divorce, I had installed many measures of security in my home, including cameras, alarm systems, and gates that locked. All of this was because of Richard's threat to "take me out." He had done everything else he promised, hadn't he? He had ruined my life and had taken away everything that was dear to me. One morning while reading my daily devotions, the printed words just engraved themselves on my heart: "I AM YOUR SECURITY SYSTEM!" God's defense was better than any way I could try to protect myself. WOW! I burst into tears asking God to forgive me for all the fear and anxiety that came from not trusting Him. I felt the sense of dread melting away and I was being filled with security and boldness. God would be my protector. I felt free from fear for the first time. Free from the bondage that was holding me back from my true purpose. I told Lee and my friends that I would go alone to talk with Richard, because God would be by my side.

I also felt led to look up the biblical meaning of the number seven. Why would God choose seven years later to send me to Richard with forgiveness? Seven was tied to God's creation and His Sabbath day of rest. It stood for completeness and perfection, both physical and spiritual. I also read that seven is an assurance that divine assistance is on the way. I was ready for both rest and divine assistance.

Lee prayed with me the night before the meeting. He asked for a peaceful night of rest and for God to have His way in the meeting. My dreams were full of peace, and I awoke ready for the day. It was not really a surprise when the pastor preached on unforgiveness that morning. He talked about holding onto offense and how "unforgiveness is like drinking poison and expecting the other person to die." I had never said "Amen" in church as much as I did to that sermon. The pastor also mentioned an "ex-husband" multiple times which caught my attention. I realized that in many ways, I had gone through the motions of forgiving, but my heart held onto the pain and torment … and the offense. I had to release it for good. The pastor ended by saying, "Make sure you don't go to bed tonight without seeing that it is done!"

Lee and I met with Calvin and Leigh for lunch and the table was buzzing about the message and how it was meant for me. Afterward, I dropped Lee off at home and headed to the coffee shop to meet Richard. Unfortunately, there were many coffee shops in that part of town, and I ended up at the wrong one. Not seeing Richard's car, I called him to confirm and found he was waiting at a coffee shop down the street. I purchased an unsweetened iced tea and headed to a strip mall where I looked again for his car without seeing it. I called him again, and he told me that the coffee shop was a stand-alone building even farther down the road. Eventually, I found the correct shop and noticed an ad for a new drink in the window called "Blonde, Blonde, Blonde." I definitely felt that sign was talking about me. Thinking of God's sense of humor, I chuckled as I entered, which lightened the load. Richard was sitting at a small corner couch with coffee in hand, and he was also chuckling about the coffee shop scavenger hunt I had been on. What an icebreaker!

After a quick greeting, I got to the point. I told Richard how I had felt a desire from the Lord to ask him for forgiveness for anything hurtful I had said or done throughout the divorce. The words flowed out so easily and sincerely. He laughed a little nervous laugh and said, "Oh Angel, that is water under the bridge so long ago." I told him that I had forgiven him many years ago, but I knew that it wasn't complete until today. The enemy tried to provoke me to anger a few times during the conversation, but the Holy Spirit kept me in peace. Richard joked around mostly, but I shared honestly how I barely made it through the divorce. I started to talk about the accusations and lies of the divorce when the Holy Spirit reminded me that I had nothing more to prove. I did not condemn

Richard but told him I was sorry that he had to live so long married to me when he wanted another life instead. He said, "Angel, it wasn't like that. I truly loved you." I wasn't going to argue with him, but it seemed insincere. I sensed he was still in a prison, masking truth and pain.

Richard switched the conversation to Victoria. She was preparing to move out of state over 40 hours away. He seemed a little happy when I mentioned that we didn't talk much. Then he talked about Libby and her intelligence. I told him that I was proud of both our daughters and excited to see what God would do with their lives. Both were going through college and moving on from the anger, bitterness, and pain of the divorce. I mentioned how I hoped that both girls would have a close relationship with God. He changed the subject again and talked about how our sitting there reminded him of sitting by the pool many years ago with our coffee and unsweetened tea. It was odd that I didn't have to think about the drinking and bad times of the past but felt peaceful talking with him. I was grateful for the answers to the prayers I had prayed for him years ago when he had been told he would surely die, because here he was, still alive and, as far as I knew, cancer-free. I could only pray he would see that God has a purpose for him still. We spent about an hour together, then he got up to leave so he could get in bed for an early morning of work. He said, "Give me a hug. It's been good to see you." I did hug him and felt an amazing release when I walked away. I told Lee about the meeting and how the encounter had played out. Little did I know, at that point, the blessings that would follow.

Chapter 16:

PEACEFUL BLESSINGS (HEALING HEART AND GOD'S BLESSINGS)

A few days before Victoria's college graduation, she called and asked me to come. I was so surprised and filled with joy. I quickly rearranged some appointments and cleared my schedule to make this a priority. I would be going alone as it was too late for Lee to schedule time off. The morning of her graduation, I began to remember other special times in her life, like her preschool graduation and her high school graduation four years before. Tears welled up in my eyes as I was suddenly transported back to her first day of kindergarten. Victoria was holding my hand and her sweet little five-year-old voice was consoling me, saying, "Mommy, it's okay." I prayed that her love for me would return.

The graduation ceremony was well-planned, and Victoria looked beautiful walking across the stage in her cap and gown. I felt so proud of her accomplishments, knowing that she also planned to get her master's degree out of state. Victoria had texted me where to meet her after the ceremony. I walked up to find her with Richard and his mother. Everyone was pleasant although the meeting was short. Richard mentioned pictures, so I offered to take one of the two of them together and then one with his mother as well. Richard offered to take one for me. He commented, "Oh Angel, this is the best photo yet; you're gonna love it!" I knew that tone and could only imagine what the picture looked like. As I expected, my hair was windblown and my eyes almost shut, but it is still a fun memory for me. Victoria and I hugged and said our goodbyes. Victoria promised to call and come by for a visit before she left for graduate school. My eyes filled with tears again as I turned her over to God as usual. I said goodbye to Richard and his mother and headed home.

After that event, I realized how much I had grown and healed from all the hurt of the past. I handled certain incidents and triggers so differently now. What once would have tormented me now just bounced off me. Lee and I laughed at the graduation picture, and he told me how proud he was of my new peace. God's love and grace, mixed with Lee's constant support, had filled me with joy and contentment.

Time was flying by, and Libby's graduation would soon be here. I had recently discovered two large bins of childhood memories from the girls. Joy rushed over me as I flipped through drawings and letters that I had saved to make scrapbooks. It just seemed I was always too busy to get any sentimental projects started. All the wonderful memories came back to me while I recalled coloring pages and sweet notes of "I love you Mommy!" I was determined to complete the scrapbooks and give them to the girls one day to bring back the good memories that had been stolen through the divorce process.

I knew it was not my responsibility to rectify every problem. It was so nice now to be able to allow God to do His job in each of our lives. I no longer tried to control and fix everything myself. I had learned that it was impossible for me to change anyone's heart or attitudes. Whenever I tried to do this, it only brought great failure and disappointment. As I looked through these little treasure boxes, I prayed for my girls. I prayed for that special relationship with God in which each girl would put her trust in Him completely. I prayed that Victoria and Libby would be filled with His joy and love and freedom as each of them moved into adulthood. I also prayed that they would each find the man that God had chosen for them. The enemy had tried to steal both my girls at birth, but God had other plans for them. He would be faithful to His promises which are "yes" and "amen."

I spoke with Libby on the phone the day before her graduation ceremony. She seemed nervous and told me that it was about Richard and me being together. I assured her that everything would be fine as we had already seen each other at Victoria's graduation. We were just getting ready for bed at the hotel when we got another call from Libby that we needed to come right away for a social on campus after baccalaureate. She hadn't been aware it was for parents. We hopped up and got dressed and met her there. I loved seeing her flit around like the social butterfly she was. We spent some time meeting her friends and supporting her. Although I was glad she wanted us there, she did seem hurt that her dad couldn't make it.

The girls' college graduations were so different for me than the two high school graduations. Now that the girls were independent, I was included and welcomed. It made me feel joyful to be invited and to participate.

After Lee and I were seated for Libby's graduation ceremony, I saw Richard and his mother sitting a few rows down. Now that I was healing, I could have true compassion for them like sheep without a shepherd. My heart wanted them both to know the love of God and seek His ways. I silently prayed for them until the music started.

My heart filled with pride to see Libby walk across the stage. Lee squeezed my hand three times which is our sign of love for each other. I felt so proud to see Libby moving forward. I was reminded of Philippians 2:13 which says, "For it is [not your strength, but it is] God who is effectively at work in you, both to will and to work [that is strengthening, energizing, and creating in you the longing and the ability to fulfill your purpose] for his good pleasure."

The graduation went smoothly, and Lee and I attended the reception afterwards. Seeing my little butterfly so happy was the highlight of the day. This was again an answer to my lifelong prayer for Libby to succeed and do well in life. I felt comforted knowing that both my girls were beginning to trust me again as they saw the changes that God had made in my life.

Lee and I went back home to work as usual. God was the head of our family. I could see that I was gaining lost ground daily through standing on God's Word. The past hurts were losing their grip on me, and I was able to love with no boundaries. I no longer lived a life of secrets. I was no longer a victim but victorious in my daily walk with the Lord. It seemed God was sending many hurting women my way who were not yet free from the oppression I had lived through. I had a great desire for others to experience the freedom God could bring to them. I used my own testimony to give them hope for their own lives.

I was changing a bulb on the porch one day when it slipped and broke into a million pieces. As I cleaned up the mess, I saw the parallel of my life that had been shattered for so long. As God began to take charge of my life and form me, He began to replace all the shattered, broken glass with a new, full life held together with vibrant unity, happiness, and joy. He was making me whole again. I was becoming a new creation, refined and restored ... a masterpiece. I no longer felt worried and anxious about tomorrow. I had everything I could need. Matthew 6:33-34 summed it up for me:

*"Seek the Kingdom of God above all else,
and live righteously, and he will give you everything
you need. So don't worry about tomorrow,
for tomorrow will bring its own worries.
Today's trouble is enough for today."*

I learned to allow others to choose their paths in life without my criticism and judgment. Just like Barabbas was set free when Jesus died on the cross for all our sins, each person is offered freedom and eternal life but must choose to accept what has been given freely. I chose life for myself, but I must allow others that freedom of choice, as well. We don't have to carry the burden of choices that others make as we can never change anyone. What we can do is spread joy, peace, love, and hope that is given to us by God. He gives us strength for this as we see in Philippians 4:13: "I can do all things through Christ which strengtheneth me."

I found joy in giving, now that I was complete. Out of my brokenness, blessing was being brought forth. I was awarded a small piece of real estate and my mausoleum during the divorce. Knowing I would never use it, I was able to help a needy family by donating the mausoleum. The family lost everything in a house fire and then lost a close family member with no money for the burial. I met them in the same room where Richard and I bought the mausoleums eight years earlier. I knew the number eight meant a "new beginning." I heard the Lord say, "Now you're blessing those who are broken." In these reflections, I see God's grace and promise. He had gone ahead of me to fight my battles. I had gained strength and wisdom. I learned to truly forgive from my soul. I knew now that

I had looked for love in all the wrong places, but had found the true love of God that I had been looking for all along. I guess maybe He really found me. He knew the end of my journey would bring me more joy than I could have imagined.

I remembered a time in my deepest, darkest despair when all my cabinets were bare, and I had no way to fill them. Now I can see the way God filled them up to overflowing without my knowing it. He also filled my heart with a love that I never thought possible. So delicately and lovingly, He mended and restored my life like a tailor making tiny, intricate stitches in a well-made coat. Through the writing of this book, God helped me to heal as I recalled events from my past. He also gave me a desire to use my testimony to help others have hope and an expectation that God is working all parts of their lives together for their good. This story was written to comfort others who are hurting and need the healing that only God's love can provide. It is not just for one, but maybe millions of brokenhearted souls. As I finished this last chapter, I sat still, praising God and listening to the words of a song by Danny Gokey. Listen to them and know, dear friend, that God isn't finished yet.

"HAVEN'T SEEN IT YET"
BY DANNY GOKEY

Please listen to the song and the lyrics.

ABOUT THE AUTHOR

 I thank God for his guidance, love, and healing most of all. I would like to thank my Momma "Margie" and Grandma "Lizzie" who now reside in Heaven and prayed so many prayers for me that carried me through life until I meet them again someday.

A special thank you to all of those who were and have always been there for me during my happy and sad days. (You will know who you are.) I can't even begin to show or tell you how much I appreciate your friendship and love and support then and now. I would like to especially thank my loving and wonderful husband Ernie Brewster for going through it all "right by my side," making me feel loved and secure. I also thank God for giving you to me! I thank you, the reader, for having the courage no matter what your circumstances or the situation you or someone you know have been in—or are in right now to pick up this up book and read and share it with all you know. I love you all.